# Situations

## THE LIES BENEATH THEM ALL

## Felicia Lynette

A Fresh Wind Publishing

# SITUATIONS

# Contents

# SITUATIONS

*The Lies Beneath Them All*

*Written By:*

*Felicia Lynette*

# Acknowledgments

First and foremost, I would like to thank my mother, who has been my rock all of my life, especially during this time. She's been my ear and a sounding board, an encourager, you name it, she's been that. And I am singing "Ain't no Mama like the one I got." A special thanks to my pops, Jeff Clark! Thanks for being solid from day one. RIP to my daddy Elisha "Chick" Brass

To my only blood sister Roz, thank you, thank you, thank you! Thank you for being radical, wanting to physically fight just as you did when we were kids. Thank you for the jewelry boxes that you constantly sent to me... When something was being stripped away you did everything in your power to try to help replace it. Thank you for all of the conversations and the daily check-ins when things got rough. A special thanks to the ones who made me an aunt Dominique and Devin; also, my little princess Ava Bug.

Next, I want to thank my daughters who, during this difficult time in my life, were also going through tragic moments of their own. However; they took the time to check on their mother and make sure I was OK. My oldest Lyshae has definitely tried to defend my name and went to bat for me publicly. Thank you, my baby girl, Kayla, who had to endure some dark moments because of the relationships that I have experienced. I want you to know that I love you both. I thank God for putting you in my life and I have enjoyed being your "mommy." You both were my reasons why and also the sacrifices at the same time.

To my Beyond The Veil Ministries Family- Words cannot express how much I love and appreciate you. Thank you for loving me as the Pastor/Apostle. Thank you for all of your prayers! Pastor Seiji, thank you for taking the lead when I could not. Thank you to the leaders and members. You all are absolutely amazing!

To the entire Bibleway Church Family and PS "Dub," thank you for accepting me initially. Many of you had no idea what I was experiencing and you did not care. You just loved me! Thank you!

What can I say to my Crunch Fitness Family? This place became my saving grace! You all put something in me that I didn't know existed, and that was dedication to a craft I thought I despised. It was during this time that I knew I could be dedicated to anything in life. My trainer and friend NA-BI-LA (Pia), man, words cannot express how thankful I am for the day we crossed paths. We had no idea that our friendship would grow to this level. Also, sometimes we are on two different journeys in our spiritual walk; as I've told you, I would take you any day over many of those that ascribe to the Christian faith. Your heart is pure and cannot be touched by most. To Piper, thank you for trusting me to be your friend and for you being my friend. You had no idea the number of days I came in ready to break and to look at Chandler's face, those days gave me hope. Thank you to such a wonderful team/family you all have been to me! I love you for life! Many of you became friends later and I will cherish that forever.

My best friend, Pastor Mario Brown, it's been 20+ years of friendship. Most of what I have written about in this book you have endured with me. You have laughed with me, and you got mad with me during the bad times. You have been the true definition of a best friend! Thank you so much for your years of friendship and love towards my girls and me!

To Latedra, aka Drop affectionately called my sister cousin best friend, I am crying as I am writing this; no words can express my gratitude for you. We have not always seen eye to eye, and I blame that on the 10 year age difference, but man, our bond is simply outstanding because of our love for each other! Although we're cousins, we are like sisters and best friends forever. I don't have to put what you are and what you mean to me in a book; just know that I love you to infinity! Thank you for being the lotus, the push when I needed it, and I wanted to give up; you would not let me. Thank you for the tears and crying with me. Thank you for the moments of helping to heal what has been destroyed. In the words of the color purple, me and you must never part my Tee Dada.

To my Chicago Pastor, Chris Harris, thank you! I always say you may not come when I want you to, but you're always on time. Thank you for hearing the words of desperation, and like any spiritual leader would come to the rescue. It's been over 20 years, and although things have changed a bit, they are still the same! I love you for life!

Thank you to my Bishop, Don G Banks Sr., for all of your love and support throughout the last seven years! I love you for life! And also, MY First Pastor Sharlaski, thank you! Thank you for always keeping me together on the outside. Thank you for speaking words of encouragement to me. I love you!

To one of my closest friends who never turned his back on me, trusted my gift from the moment he met me, Bishop Michael D. Douglas Sr. Words cannot express how much I appreciate you. I love you for life!

To my Goddaughter and graphic designer Antoinette and Moore's Graphic Designs. Thank you for all that you do! Thank you for being consistent! No more matchmaking for you.

Thank you to my wonderful friend "Blue" for being an ear, and thanks to your entire legal team.

To my very new family RIM and Apostle and Lady Bobby Stapleton words cannot express how happy and fulfilled I am since you all have allowed me to hang around. Just know it was just what I needed.

To my wonderful and amazing Marketing and Media Strategist, publicist and end all be all, Marcie Wilson, You are the best! I was praying for you and I was stuck. You came right in and did what I needed.

Thank you to Curt McAfee for your professionalism with every photo shoot. Also, Britiney Hodges for being my make up artist for the photo shoot.

Lastly, To every reader that will take the time to read every page;

THANK YOU!

Cover photo (Front and Back) Curt McAfee - Ridgeland MS
Cover Design Moore's Graphics - Monroe LA

# Endorsement

As believers we're always searching for answers concerning the events of our lives. We struggle to know the secrets that produce a wholesome and fulfilling life. Too often we find ourselves hiding or masking ourselves in church because we refuse to be transparent or truthful about our life happenings. It takes courage to address what we try to mask or hide. Pastor Felicia has gone where few Christians dare to go. She addresses her life issues with integrity by looking in the mirror. That's right... she discovered it wasn't everybody else; it was her. I applaud and admire her boldness to confront self. It is one of our most challenging endeavors in life. This book not only focuses on her mistakes but she provides spiritual remedies that bring healing and happiness.

God calls everyone to a ministry purpose and it's our life pursuit to find it through His love and grace. Felicia Smith reveals her call to help the hurting, lost, confused and broken. If you are like most believers, you want to know the secrets and solutions to living your best life. You will be blessed by what she shares in this writing. It is definitely anointed by God. I challenge you to take a BOLD look inside and you too will be liberated by the power of God. THIS IS A MUST READ!

Bishop Dr. Don G. Banks
UFCCM Southwest Jurisdictional Bishop
Dean of Sacred College of Bishops
Senior Pastor – The Greater Realness Cathedral

# Forward

The McMillian Dictionary defines the word situation as *"the set of conditions that exist at a particular time in a particular place"*. Through a broad and transparent lens, Felicia has revealed "situations" in her life that have at times been awkward, complicated, and complex.

This body of work takes you on a private journey familiar to many but rarely expressed publicly. With the courage of a warrior, Felicia sheds religious cloaks that inadvertently breeds shame and judgment and pours her soul out like a river of living water.

I believe that **Situations: What Lies Beneath** will not only start healing for many but, in many ways, help the reader give personal permission to their heart, soul, and mind to heal and finally be free of obstructive and debilitating behaviors that work against their authenticity and purpose.

This book has the feel of "that special aunt" sitting with her nieces, sharing painful yet liberating truths about her past mistakes and victories, all the while praying and hoping that perhaps something she says would prevent them from making those same mistakes.

I believe the most significant takeaways from this book are:

- Accept the challenge to confront your historical context and content and make a choice to never live beneath your privilege and authenticity.
- Never substitute who you are for what you need.
- Recognize that you deserve to live above and not beneath anyone or anything.

-Pastor Mario C. Brown
Senior Pastor, The Kingdom Church,


**Auburn, AL**

# Preface

This book was written out of experiences that I've endured. Whether you've been in a relationship, marriage, or have family situations, this book will definitely add value to your life. It can help with the healing process of any journey you are on..

If you just read this book as an exciting novel and learn about my life, you are missing the point. However, there are fascinating stories that you will read. They will be pretty informative. This book communicates how I entered situations I shouldn't have been in, how I escaped, and how I healed. All of these situations will have you shedding tears, having moments of laughter, and may even deal with stored-up anger that you need to get free from. I encourage you to journal while reading and write down the areas in your life where you can do things differently.

# INTRODUCTION

**SITUATIONS**

*THE LIES BENEATH THEM ALL*

I describe a situation as something you get into because of the need to be rescued. At 53 years old, four failed marriages, and four additional engagements, I finally decided to step back and look at myself. When you are forced to look at yourself, some of the things you see are great, and some are not so great. I'd like to think that not meeting my father until I was 18 had a lot to do with decisions I made throughout my entire life.

Today, I am looking at matters of the heart. Imagine never being in love. I know what you're thinking, how is that possible after four marriages? The truth of the matter is there was ***a form of love***, but what kind of love was it?

This book is about failed marriages/relationships and more about being stuck in situations. One after the other, we all find ourselves in a situation or two. It doesn't matter who you are or your walk of life; they occur. How do we get out of them? What I am learning is to focus more on how it happened more than how to get out. If we face the harsh reality of what made us enter that door in the first place, the quicker the healing can take place.

The truth of the matter is, where I have placed the blame on so many others, a lot of what I experienced were things I could have avoided if I only had paid attention to the signs that were before me. I believe that as you read this book, it will be more than just you reading my story and seeing the characters but you will see the signs that were ignored. You will also see a life-changing, life-altering, and mind-blowing awakening and healing. My prayer is that you will see the signs early and never enter those doors.

For so many years I tried to be perfect for everyone else that I was failing at being the best me for me. I plan to be as transparent as I can be. I started the idea of writing this book years ago, and I could not write it. The problem was I wasn't ready to be transparent. I wasn't prepared to look at myself. Having to face my flaws was very difficult for me to do. It is easy to walk around with our masks and perfect made-up selves and hide from the world. But when you have to look at yourself, you can't hide the truth. When we are messed up, we are truly messed up! The lifestyle I lived made me believe I couldn't have flaws. So, with my imperfect self, I put on a façade for others. I no longer want to fake the funk; I no longer want to hide my imperfections. The fact is I was messed up, and daily, God is revealing me to me. At one point, I thought that living transparently wasn't an option until I realized that living transparently was my only option.

As you read this book, I hope that you see my imperfections and how I overcame them as a sign that you, too, can overcome any obstacle you face. Some situations aren't as intense as others, but they are necessary to tell so you can recognize patterns. Fasten your seatbelts; it's going to be a rocky ride.

***Before we begin,***

- Pray and ask God to open your eyes so that you can see toxic patterns.

- Think about the broken relationships in your life and what red flags you may have missed.
- Grab a journal! As you read, jot down your takeaways as we journey through situations.

***Disclaimer: To protect the identity of others, no names were used in this book.***

# SITUATION 1



*GETTING OUT OF THE NEST*

This part of my life is called "situations." Today, I realized I have never been in love with four failed marriages and four other engagements. This was a hard pill to swallow, considering I got married for reasons I thought were all about love. At the end of every relationship, I asked the question, "How did I get here?" The fact of the matter is, I believe in the institution of marriage and everything it stands for. I was great at picking "boyfriends" but horrible at seeing they should never have been more than that.

One of the things I had to come to grips with was in every relationship I had committed to, I was a wife before becoming a wife. I gave a lot of myself! I cooked, I cleaned, I listened attentively, I spoke with affirmations, I pushed them to excel and made them see their next even before they knew what their next was. But there was still something missing for me. I gave and gave and gave, and often I was empty with no one to be for me what I was with them.

*Don't expect more out of others than they are capable of giving. This makes you settle, while knowing that it isn't enough.*

The "situation" in my first marriage was, I wanted to get out of my mother's home like most young adults. I was 20 with a one-year-old daughter and he was 34. I now know the 14 year age difference was too huge. He was my second relationship with a 14 year age difference. My daughter's father was also 14 years older than me. I had told myself I was mature. I said to myself that I didn't like boys my age; they were too immature for me; So older was the way for me. The fact of the matter was I didn't grow up knowing my father. I was looking for a love that only a father could give. I met my father when I was 18, and all of my young adult life, I thought I needed someone older when in reality, I just needed my daddy. The little girl in me was at constant war with the young adult I had become. I decided I was grown and I needed to leave my mother's house. I made bad decisions early on to date and have intimate relationships with older men.

The man I married rescued me from my mother's house. So, of course, I loved him, right? You've heard the saying two grown women cannot live together. I thought I was grown, but I wasn't developed enough to live on my own. I needed to be rescued! So along comes this man, two months after I had broken up with my daughter's father. He was handsome, dressed well, always smelled good, and had his own business. We met at church, and our church was very small, so imagine, all of the single women were trying to get his attention, but he was interested in me. We dated for a few months, and then married shortly thereafter. This was the start of my cycle of marriages.

He lived in the basement of his mother's house, because he had just left a failed marriage. I found out later he had three failed marriages. I am not usually one to talk a lot about a transference, but we must watch who we are connected to and make sure their past lives don't interfere with our present or future lives. I was too young to realize what I wanted and needed in a relationship. After all, how well did I know myself? We had no romance, but he gave me the security I wanted and the ability to look like everyone else around me that was getting married. There are times we watch those around us and secretly coveted what they had. Little did I know, most of them were miserable but covered it up with church and The Bible. With no romance, there also was no official proposal. I came in from work one day, and there was a JCPenney jewelry box on the dresser. He was asleep because he had been working all day. When I came in, he said, *"look on the dresser."* I was so excited! Finally, a solution to my situation. Excited wasn't the word to describe what I felt. I was about to be married at almost 21 and live in my own home.

I planned a wedding to take place within the next few months. What was the rush? I had a situation and I needed it to be rectified! He fulfilled that situation, only it wasn't as great as I thought it would be. After the wedding, there was no honeymoon, and it didn't matter; he resolved my situation. We moved into the home that belonged to him and his ex-wife. On this day, I found out he had been married three times prior. A lot of emotions took place when I found that out. Was I making the biggest mistake of my life? Was my mom right? She didn't come to my wedding because she said "The Lord told her not to." Her decision devastated me, but it didn't stop me from proceeding. I remember preparing to get married, and my sister pulled me to the side to tell me my mother wasn't coming. I was mad and hurt, but I went ahead with my plans. I remember getting to the door to walk down the aisle, asking myself: *"what would this look like if I just ran away?"* I feel like this is where my life started to spin out of control. I knew I shouldn't get married. I had spent my last $1,200 on a wedding gown that I couldn't afford. All of these people were in attendance, and what would they think? Would it look too much like the movie Runaway Bride? So I walked down the aisle and told myself I was happy and could make this last forever.

We got married and spent the first night in the house that belonged to him and someone else. The second day of being in that home he was frustrated because he had to return to work for someone else because his business had failed. He blamed me for his newly found problems. *"If I hadn't married you, I would still have my business."* I was devastated! How could the man that loved me speak to me in this manner? I continued on cooking because I hated arguments. Cooking was my mechanism for coping in life.

Late that afternoon, we made love before he had to go to work. When he left for work, he said to lock the door, but I fell asleep. When he got off work that next morning the door was still unlocked. He came in and accused me of leaving it open for my ex to sneak in. As puzzled as I was, I continued throughout the day to avoid arguments. Later on, the fight continued. I was sitting on the living room floor changing the radio station, and I looked up, and he grabbed me by the throat and dragged me all across the floor. With tears in my eyes, I looked up at him, and I cried hard! I had never been in an abusive relationship before. But there were so many against us that I couldn't walk away. According to them, we were never supposed to make it due to our age difference. I knew I should have left, but go where? Back to my mom's? This situation had just rescued me from there. On my own? I had no concept of paying bills or living alone. So I stayed because I was just rescued. But was I really?

For the next four years, I endured lousy sex and a very verbally abusive relationship. I thought I was hurt with the physical abuse, but the verbal abuse did a lot more damage. He said awful things like; I was ugly, no one else would want me, and I would never amount to anything. When you hear these things, you almost begin to believe there is some truth to it.

After being in this place for five years, the thing that I feared finally happened, I was fed up! I had held my tongue for five years for fear he would hit me. I couldn't talk about the lousy sex or that I was unhappy. I would ask God, "*am I going to have to live with this kind of sex for the rest of my life?*" Whew! I thought! I was only 25; I still have a lot of living to do. Do I have an affair? I thought, do I leave? Or do I tell him that I'm not satisfied? Oh, I told him alright, Right when he was making his move to start the sex. I yelled, "*I am tired of having 2 minutes worth of sex. Why don't you save it all up for one day per week to last longer?"* I had shattered his feelings. It was hurtful, and I knew it. From that moment on, we were never the same. We argued, screamed, and cursed each other daily. I was no longer biting my tongue, and he couldn't take me speaking out. Then one day, he had enough of me speaking back to him that he slapped me so hard that I hit the floor.

I left the house for one month. He begged me to come back and stated he would commit to counseling, one session down, and he decided he didn't need it. I said, OK, but if you hit me one time, I would leave and never come back. Well, a couple of weeks later, it happened. It was a push down on the bed once I spoke my mind. Although he did not hit me, I knew enough about abuse to know it would not end there. I had watched my mom be in an abusive marriage, and my grandparents fought often. Once you begin to accept their anger in this manner, it gets worse. First a push, or a drag across the floor, and before you know it, you're covering up a black eye with make-up, or worse, you're dead. None of which I wanted, and I had enough to leave. I left! I was done. I had a girlfriend, who had a duplex, and she allowed me to stay there rent-free until I saved enough money to get my place. It wasn't in the best neighborhoods, and had I not been in this "situation," I would never move there on my own. Gunshots every night is all we heard. But I was peaceful with my daughter and away from stress.

Once I got an apartment of my own, right when the divorce was about to be final, he came there drunk and begged me not to leave. I was scared that he wanted to fight again. I stood my ground, and we were divorced.

The situation didn't end there. I had baggage! I had bought into the words that no one would want me, that I was ugly and wouldn't amount to anything. I believed it! I believed it so much that I made a bold statement that I would do to/with men what they have done to and with us. I would sleep with anyone I wanted to, hang with anyone that I wanted to. I had no self-love, I had no confidence in who I was. I even belittled myself and slept with married men. I was adding more damage to myself. I had gotten into this marriage for a situation but I found myself not making me better, but worse. I believed the words that were spoken that I lived it out. The abuse that I lived through for five years, I began to live it out in sex. For the next three years of my life, I tortured myself. Until one day, God snapped me into reality and said no more.

For the next five years, I lived a celibate life and rebuilt my purpose to who God made me. To get over the words that I had bought into, God told me every time I would pass a mirror, speak positive affirmations and tell myself how beautiful I was. I was reminded of how God saw me. He told me not to tell anyone why I was doing this. Others around me thought I was vain, but I was merely trying to get healed. It took one year of me affirming my worth to change what I believed about myself. I learned to guard my heart and not allow other people's opinions to matter to me. It was a rough road because even though I saw myself differently, a part of me always wondered how others were viewing me.

Finally, this situation was over!!

**Journal Entry**

- What red flags have you ignored in your relationships?
- What bad behavior have you adopted because of bad relationships?
- In your journal, jot down at least 3 affirmations and speak them to yourself for the next 7 days.

# SITUATION 2



*THE COVER-UP FOR THE CHURCH*

Finally, I was healed and living my best life. Working in ministry for the last five years, I was celibate and being a great mommy! Then one day, I was ministering at a conference. My title was "Living Single, Saved and Satisfied!" It was great! The lives of the people were being changed based upon the information they were receiving. Afterward, there was a guy that attended the church. He was 6'2, dark complexion, and bald. Whew, I thought, *"he looks good!"* We talked for a bit. He said he worked construction, we exchanged conversation, and he asked me out. I hadn't been out in a while, but what was it going to hurt? It's just dinner. Dinner turned into a conversation back at my apartment, and one thing led to another. After we finished, I noticed the condom came off on the inside of me, and we were stuck pulling it out. I jumped up and said, *"I'm pregnant."* He asked how I knew; I jokingly said I am very fertile; I can get pregnant if you look at me wrong. I was taught after you are done preaching, you are the most vulnerable. Why didn't I pay attention to the signs? Why didn't I just say no? I was thinking, Fe, here you go again.

I was moving the following weekend to a condo, and he said he and his friends would help me move. I didn't talk to him all week because I realized I didn't like him, and I was upset with myself for breaking my celibacy with someone I barely knew and didn't like. He didn't show up to help me move, and I knew I never had to see him again Until two months passed by, and I realized I had no monthly cycle. I called him and told him I was pregnant.

***And this is how Situation 2 begins.***

I was a preacher and a leader in the church. There was no way I could be pregnant and not married. In my mind, we had to get married; that was the only way out. But I didn't like him like that; I wasn't in love with him, how can I do that? I had to learn to love him for him being able to get me out of this situation. I had to save face for the church's sake. Here I was about to get married, knowing I wasn't in love. He had already shown me a side of him that I knew wasn't what I needed in a spouse. And just like that, we got married. We didn't have a big wedding, and we had a family potluck reception.

He moved into the condo with me, and it was crazy. He barely came home. When he did come home, it was very late at night. I found out the construction job he had was the first job he had ever worked, and he was a reformed "street dude." How did this happen? I am usually more in tune before connecting with someone.

It was now wintertime, and the construction work was slow. Instead of finding a job that pays, he would rather sit and wait with no income. He wouldn't help pay bills, he was staying out all night, and when the time came he wanted to fight. What? Because I found out there were other women, All I was thinking was you're not going to pay bills, hang out all night, cheat, and now you want to fight. What?! Later, there was an apology. I didn't want to end the marriage because I was pregnant. I decided to work it out. The time came for me to have the baby. Where was my husband? What am I going to do? It was 2 AM, and I was having contractions. I got up and drove myself to the hospital. I left a note for my daughter and goddaughter to take a taxi to the hospital if I wasn't back. I know I could have called him and said I'm in labor, but why? If you know you have a pregnant wife in the last month of the pregnancy, there's no way you should be away at 2 AM.

My daughter called his sister, and she eventually told him, and he showed up at the hospital. This situation I was in made me feel less than the woman I knew I was. God called me to greatness; why did I allow this situation to overtake my life? I couldn't focus on that because I had a beautiful baby girl on the way. It was Easter Sunday morning, and she was born. I was so happy with her that nothing else mattered. She was pretty as a button. I stared at her pretty regularly, in amazement at her beauty.

Things were OK for a couple of days, and then they were not. The arguing started, disappearing, coming in late, you name it. But I was so focused on this pretty little bundle of joy that I had and ignored that he had returned to his regular habits. Then one day, I woke up, and it hit me that he had not been home all night. I packed his clothes and set them outside. When he finally returned and noticed his things outdoors, he was immediately upset. He came in arguing, fussing, pushing and shoving, wanting to fight. My oldest daughter grabbed the baby screaming out loud *"I hate you, I hate you"*. I knew that it was time for him to go. I remember thinking I never wanted to be a single parent again. I hadn't been working, and the condo was getting too expensive, so I moved into an apartment. Once again, he begged and tagged along and asked if he could come. I allowed it because I was still dealing with the same situation. We worked out an agreement for bills; we would split all of the accounts down the middle. I remembered thinking how people stayed in marriages full of cheating and fighting. I don't know how to do this. But I was too young for another divorce.

I started back working, leaving early in the morning and returning late in the evenings. I gave my half of the rent for two months and told him to put it with his half and take it to the rental office. That was not happening. I had no idea until the rental office called me and stated that the sheriffs were there and set all of my furniture outside one day. What!? I was outraged! What do you mean by putting everything outside? As it turns out, I was giving him the money, but he was not turning in the money to the rental office. He was home during the day, so each notice that they put on the door, he snatched it off, and I never knew. I knew at that moment I was now finally done, no more comebacks, no more anything. I left work immediately and got a moving truck and loaded all of the furniture. The rental agent stated that she was going to sit outside with my belongings until I got there. She said, your things are too nice; if I don't sit out here, they will be gone. I arrived later, loaded everything on the moving truck, and immediately took it to storage. I moved back in with my mother. As I sat in her living room, I thought how ironic, the very place that situation one rescued me from was the exact location I'm ending up now.

*If you do not deal with the issues properly, you will find yourself facing those same issues again.*

And now this situation was entirely over, and I was heading to situation three. It was an eye-opener. My mother had purchased a building to move her daycare center into, and above the building was a three-bedroom apartment—just enough space for my daughters and me to start over.

**Journal Entry:**

- Identify those situations you covered up because you were afraid of what others would say?
- What issues have you NOT dealt with? What have you been running from?
- Name 3 people you are grateful for? My mother had a place for me to stay. She was there when I needed her most.

# SITUATION 3



We are some "hoes." One of my favorite late aunts would say to the women in our family pretty regularly. She was one of two of my dad's last sisters remaining. She had a way with words that would make us laugh all of the time. But that statement resonates in our heads almost daily as we laugh at things that she had said. However, if you hear something too long, you start wondering if there is some truth to that. Two failed marriages, and now I'm starting over. Each time I came out of a failed marriage, I found myself returning to the place that wanted to do men the way men do us. Not a great way to live, and it did not show healing. But instead, it showed revenge! After each situation, all I could think of is to protect my heart and get back at others!

> *When we allow bad things to enter our hearts,*
> *it comes back twice as strong.*

This time was worse! I was still in church, still loving God, but a secret life is what I called this one. I did not want to be in a serious relationship at this time, but I did not want to be alone! I spent time with people I should not have spent time with, husbands that were not mine, and sometimes multiple partners! I started telling myself I was addicted to sex! I'm still not sure if that was true or not but what I do know is, things had gotten to an all-time high. Sometimes it would be extreme, and then other times, I would just lay low. I finally got to the place where I started dating again seriously, but I still saw other people! This created an error in my life that the people I would enter into serious relationships with the sex would be horrible, but they looked good, fit who I was publicly, but were nothing of what I needed privately! So I began to live a double life. I would date and be "church" celibate with the person I'm seriously dating because I wanted and needed them to see me as a good girl, but I would have sexual relationships in my private time away from them.

I remember getting into a serious relationship, and it was long distance. I met him through my 1st cousin, who I affectionately call my sister-cousin- best friend. I started traveling back-and-forth to visit him and it was great for a while. Then it was time for sex. He flew my oldest daughter and I to town and we stayed at his home. It was the most amazing weekend ever. He catered to me, wined, and dined me; it was great, and did I mention the sex was phenomenal! Finally! Someone I'm in a relationship with, and the sex is excellent. All I thought about was I no longer had to live a double life. I was happy this was great, and this was my turning point.

One day he decided to visit me in Chicago. I was excited because he was coming to my hometown to meet my friends and my pastor. That meant a lot to me because those were some of my most incredible friends. Because of the industry I worked in, I was able to get him an excellent suite downtown at the Chicago Palmer House Hilton. He asked if his best friend could come along so that while I'm at work, he would have things to do. I was OK with that. There was a lot going on that weekend. My daughter had concerts, and we all had planned on attending. I kept the key to the hotel room just because it was in my name. Also, we were dating, so I knew that I would probably spend some time there. After being in town one night, I arrived at the hotel the next day around 3:00 PM. He and his best friend had gone shopping. I entered the hotel room, and very typical of a man, his clothes are on the floor, so I started picking them up. I also pulled up the sheets on the bed, and as I was straightening the bed, I saw a brown stain on the sheets. I looked, and it did not look good. I took a sniff, and it smelled like someone had defecated on the sheets. I immediately got sick to my stomach. I went into the bathroom and found all types of lubricant on the toilet. This could only mean one thing, the man that I thought was perfect and would keep me from living a double life also had a double life. I never confronted him; I never addressed it. I just exited the relationship quietly. Although I continued with the weekend plans, it was clear that I had checked out of the relationship.

We went to the concert, we hung out with my church family, and it was at that moment, every one of my church friends said, you cannot possibly be dating him; he looks suspect. If you hung around us and you knew what "suspect" meant. He had a double life! This was confirmation, and I knew it. When I got him back to the airport, I no longer talked to him in a way that either one of us would consider us as dating. So now I'm back to square one, treating men like they treat us and living a double life that tormented me. I was still preaching; I was still singing; I was still worshiping God and a great leader in our church. All I could think of is if anyone saw this part of me, they would disown me. It had gotten out of hand. I was back living up to that statement that my aunt made of us *we are some hoes.*

I was so frustrated with myself that I tried to run away from myself. My oldest daughter had moved to New York for college, and it was just the baby and me. I thought I needed to leave Chicago. That was my answer to get away from that city and all of my problems. So, I moved to TX. My sister-cousin-best friend and her husband flew to Chicago, rented a car, and drove me to Dallas with my clothes during a horrible snowstorm. This was it. I was going to start over and leave all of the shameful living behind me. I lived there for a couple of months, and I knew it was not time for me to leave Chicago. As frustrating as it was, I had to go back and face what I started. One of my best friends and co-laborers in the church came to Dallas by car and picked me up as she, too, knew it wasn't time. When I got back, I was dealing with the same problems, issues, and situations! Back to the sexual addiction back to the multiple partners, except now it has gotten worse. The various partners consisted of not just men but now men and women! I needed help, and I needed God to help me.

During this time, my oldest daughter had called to share a part of her life with me. She was about 19 at the time and had become very independent. We were estranged from the ages of 16 to 19 and now became best friends. We went from mom; you don't understand, to suddenly, my opinions mattered. I was happy that we were finally at that place. But what she was getting ready to share, I was not prepared to hear. When you raise your children, you expect them to grow up, get a college degree, get a great job, enjoy life, save money, keep their credit straight, one day get married, and have children. All of a sudden, that boat was sinking. She said to me, *"Mom, I don't know how you're going to take this, but I need to tell you anyway".* I said "It's OK; you can tell me anything, I can handle it". She continued: *"I've decided that I'm at a place in my life that I believe I like women; I think I always have and didn't know how to interpret it".* I was quiet; I did not know what to say. I did not want her to feel like she could not trust me to love her no matter what. *"Are you sure, Pookie!?"* Hoping that it would be an April fools joke or some prank, but it wasn't. This was her reality and her life. Immediately I said, *"if that's your decision I love you anyway."*

When we got off the phone, it bothered me. I cried for weeks. I still went on with my life as I usually would; Work, home, church, home, and whatever was leftover. All I could think of was how could this happen? That is not the way I raised her! We know better than this! The Church world taught us that when someone doesn't do things the way we feel they should, because of the way that we've interpreted the Bible, we should ostracize them. But that was my baby! No way was I prepared to walk away from my child! I remember sitting on the front row at the church, and my pastor, as he was praying for people, came over to me to pray for me and said God said that's enough! Come out of the depression; you've raised your daughter to be the best her that she could be. Her life now it's up to her to live it as she sees fit. God will get us through this. Something about hearing those words in that setting shifted and altered me. It was as if God himself had said them, and I sat up straight at attention, saying; *"Yeah, Fe you got this!"* This was a situation that I was not going to allow to harden me. After all, what heaven or hell did I have to put her in with all that I had going on?

I was still dealing with my own mess. There was one partner that I could never shake; I could never say no, whatever they wanted, I did; whenever they wanted it, I did it and however, they wanted it, I did it! One evening after a church service at about 10:30 or 11:00 PM, we would sit upstairs after church for hours, eat, crack jokes, and laugh! But this particular night, I needed to leave. There was one person I was addicted to, and we made plans to meet up. However, my pastor and the assistant pastor wouldn't allow me to leave when I wanted to. I stood up; it was about midnight. *"Alright, everyone, I'll talk to you later. Girl, where are you going? Sit down; we're not done! You all I got to go to work in the morning it's getting late. Sit down, girl, we're not done."* I laughed and laughed and sat back down. However, the minute one of them went to the restroom; I ran out of there. I had someone meeting me at home, and I wanted to get to them that night. I drove home quickly because I was getting home later than I initially told them. I wasn't worried, they had a key to let themselves in. To my surprise, when I walked in, not only was he there, but he had a guest, and it was a female. He told me he had a surprise, but the last thing I was thinking of was another woman in my home. *What's going on? I told you I had a surprise baby. What kind of surprise is another woman in my house?* *"Let me talk to you for a moment", he said. "I thought we would try something different."* I responded, *"What do you mean by something different? What is this about?"* He urged me to just trust him. Now I'm putting two and two together. *Oh wait, you want us all to be in sexual relations together. "Yeah, baby, let's try it!"* I knew I had just hit rock bottom, but I couldn't tell him no. But even this was crossing the line! I agreed to do it but I told him there will not be any interaction between her and me. The exchange will be just with you and her and you and me. He agreed although that is not what he had in mind. He knew he had to take me slowly if he ever wanted to get me there. The night lasted all night, and it was great!

When the night ended, I had so many messages from my pastor and assistant pastor asking why I had to leave so early, and no one gave me permission to leave. They were laughing, but that was the dynamic of our friendships. We would always leave at the same time. I should have waited because this time opened up doors that I never wanted to see. I even called off from work the next day. I remember crying and screaming, frustrated with myself, throwing pillows around the room, and angry at myself. How could I let myself get to this point? I knew I needed a way of escape. However, this person had a stronghold over me that I could not explain. But I knew the only way I would break free was to leave, but I knew it had to be right so I would not return, and it had to be God! But not before a few more of those nights took place. I knew God wasn't pleased, and neither was I. I would leave those moments feeling nasty, showering for hours at a time, crying, and screaming. But I couldn't understand, if I was so unhappy, why did I do it?

I was in another situation that I needed to be free of. In public, I looked perfect. I was always well dressed in the best clothes; my hair was always on point, my make-up was together, and my nails and feet were perfectly manicured. Nothing was ever out of place in public. I would sing well and orchestrate service and preach at engagements. I was the perfect person; however, I was a mess behind closed doors, and no one knew it but me. I was dying! I heard the voice of God say, **"*if you don't quit, you will die!*"** I did not know why I was destroying myself!

I sat at my desk at work one day, and my aunt called. It was June 2008. She started telling me of things going on with my dad, and I needed to come to Louisiana to help him out. I was barely making ends meet, so I could not afford a plane ticket or just jump up and leave work. She mentioned her godson was going through a rough time, and she wishes she could find him a good woman. She immediately said, "hold on, sister", (That was my nickname.) She clicked over and put us on a three-way.

*Hey Sister, are you here? Yes ma'am! Godson? Yes, ma'am. Listen here, both of you are single and good people; I may as well connect you all.* We began to chat, *How are you, sister? I'm doing well. How are you? I am well! So are you originally from Chicago? No, I'm from Gilbert, Louisiana, originally! Oh wow, that's my old stomping ground; who are your people there? The Ellis's in Gilbert; oh wow, my grandmother is best friends with an Ellis in Gilbert! Wait, was this your nickname? the one and only! I remembered him being very popular. Oh wow! We grew up together and got baptized together. This is such a small world! How do you know my aunt? She's my godmother. She and my mother were best friends. Wow, that's unbelievable. So when are you coming back to Louisiana to visit? I'm not sure that is what my aunt and I were discussing. I need to get there to check on some things with my dad. So what's the hold-up? Well, the tickets are kind of expensive for me to get there right away. What's your email address?* As I proceeded to give it to him, he said, hold on for one moment. *OK, check your email. Oh my God, you did not just send me a ticket! Yes, I did; it's for the Fourth of July, so get here, and we will figure the rest out when you're here.*

I thought in my mind, never in my wildest dreams had that ever happened to me. I was in awe!! As we continued to talk, it was time for me to go back to work. "Can I call you later? Absolutely! I said with excitement. He told Bettye thanks for the click. (*That became a joke between the three of us*) We laughed and ended the call.

Leading up to the departure date, we talked every day for hours at a time. We talked about what we did for a living and what we were aspiring to do. Talking about the future was so refreshing for me. The interesting thing is that I was dating someone. Someone I had recently met at my girlfriend's wedding, he was OK, but he was not Felicia. However, he was preparing to propose and purchase a new home for us to start a future. The fourth of July was a big day for him and his family. So telling him that I was going out of town on that day did not sit well with him.

The time had come for the trip. My airplane was to arrive at about 8:00 PM. It was a Tuesday night. We made plans that I would fry chicken; of course, everyone loves my fried chicken. My aunt had the greens going, and we were going to eat well. It seemed strange that I would be cooking at the first gathering, but what I learned from situation #1 is that cooking was my coping mechanism. So since this would be somewhat uncomfortable because I am an introvert, I decided to do what would make me comfortable. I didn't realize it then, but I was setting the tone once again. I would perform wifely duties way before the relationship developed into an actual relationship.

He was picking me up from the airport, and it was going to be my first time laying my physical eyes on him. I did not know what to expect as we were children when we last saw each other. I remember my aunt asking me how tall I was over the phone and then saying, *"well, everybody is the same height lying down"*. I didn't think much of it until he arrived at the airport. He had sent a picture, so I knew what he looked like. I get off the plane, and there I see this man with the face of the picture and body of a 5'3" man. I was so disappointed because I'm 5'7". I'm quickly turned off. He honestly didn't meet my standards. *Well, hello, sister! It's great to see you. Hi, and it's great to see you as well"*, as we embrace with a hug.

We go out to get in his huge, big body, white truck, probably the prettiest truck I have ever seen. We get in, and I'm immediately quiet. I remember telling myself, Felicia, don't act funny, Felicia, don't act funny, Felicia, don't act funny! Over and over and over and overall because he was short and much shorter than I was. Even on a casual day, I dress up and wear 5-inch heels. That's all I could think of. But we had made plans for this beautiful weekend and a fantastic welcoming Fourth of July party that they had planned for me, so I had to get it together quickly.

I went inside, greeted everyone in the home, all of my family, and they were so happy to see me. I immediately started cooking. I had to get myself together. He walks up behind me and hugs me. *Are you OK? Yes, I am!* I had talked myself into being OK and to relax. It's only a few inches. Deal with it. But once again, here I was sacrificing something important to me for the sake of someone else. I got over it and we laughed and talked all night. We talked so much leading up to the trip that I was already very connected to him. My heart was there, so I ignored the height issue and enjoyed a fabulous weekend. At the Fourth of July picnic, my dad said, "*sister, don't you have any flat shoes*". I laughed and thought nothing of it. But everyone was concerned about my height. By then, I had resolved that height wasn't an issue, and we were OK. He showed me a wonderful time! Showed me all around the town, we went to church together, and we enjoyed the weekend. Then it was time to go, and we were both sad.

That Monday, I got on a plane to head back to Chicago. I remember getting on the plane but feeling uneasy. By now, we realize we loved each other. I didn't want to go, and he did not want me to go. I sat on the plane, and I wondered how a fairytale would look if I ran to the front and said, let me off. What the heck? I thought I'm doing it! *Hey, can you guys let me off? I changed my mind? I want to get off the plane! Let me off the plane! And get my bag from underneath.* After a little bit, they allowed me to get off, and they got my bag. I called him and said *"have you left the airport yet?" "No, I'm still sitting in my car in disbelief that you are going." The funny thing is I'm not gone, come back and get me."* It was such a fairytale moment, and I have never done that before in my life, it was exciting.

He came back and got me in the truck, and I said it just didn't seem right to leave today. I felt like we had not settled things yet. That weekend we talked about moving to Louisiana, and I said I would never do that and I'm not married. That night we talked and talked about plans, marriage, and moving. It was settled, and I was moving back in August, the very next month. Now I felt like I could leave. I needed to get a resolution for the weekend. We had a plan, and I felt the happiest. And here begins Situation #4. I was headed into another chapter of life, and I wasn't free from the other life; I just ran to escape.

### Journal Entry

- What negative words has someone spoken over your life?
- Now replace those negative words with a Word from the Lord.
- Identify your own toxic behavior and devise a plan to become better

# SITUATION 4



*RUNNING AWAY*

I went back home to get things together, after all, the move date was only one month away! I was excited, but I was nervous as ever. I had so many loose ends to tie up, and this was a very abrupt move. Since I was eight years old, I had not lived in the south, and now I am returning at age 40.

The things we get ourselves into, but at some point in life, we must face them. I was now in two relationships. The one in Chicago and the one in Louisiana. However, I was committed to marriage if I moved to the one in Louisiana. Therefore, I had to have a serious conversation with the guy in Chicago. What was that going to look like, sound like, or be like? In addition, I was extremely committed to my church and had a very prominent position as a leader. That, too, was going to be a complicated conversation and an emotional one as well. I had the easy one first. I put my one-month notice in at work. The next step was to have a conversation with the guy I was in a relationship with. He made it a little easy because I did not have gas money to get home one day, and my car was in the parking garage. When I called him and told him, he said OK, he would be there before I got off work. The time came for me to get off work, and he had not shown up yet. I had to leave my car in the garage overnight and catch a ride with someone else. I was not happy. However, it made me feel like I was making the right decision, or was I?

He was a preacher and aspiring to be a pastor one day. At one time, all I wanted to do was marry a pastor, so that made my dating choices limited to who I would date. He sent me a recording of him preaching once, and I remember falling asleep on it, and when I woke up, there was a lot of loud screaming. I remember saying there's no way I could support this as his wife. It was not the kind of preaching I was used to. So I had a lot of dynamics as to why he and I would not work. His children antagonizing my daughter was a final straw for me. All of these factors helped me make the decision and go with the Louisiana guy.

**The Talk....**

He had planned a dinner at his home a couple of days after I was stranded. I knew this was the day that I would be ending us. He and I were not engaged in physical sex. However, he like to engage in foreplay, and he told himself that was OK as long as we saved ourselves from the actual act of sex until marriage. Interesting concept! Most church folks tell themselves that they are celibate if they participate in foreplay, oral sex, or some form of masturbation. It is still sex!

Dinner was amazing! But I knew we needed to talk, and I needed to relieve the pressure.

*So how was your trip? It was good! I enjoyed myself, and I got everything straight that I needed to get straight with my dad. Oh, that's great. You know I was a little upset with how you sprung on me that you were going out of town. I'm sure, but we do what we have to do for our loved ones, and my dad needed me. As a result, I've decided to move to Louisiana. What? How could you make such a decision without communicating with me first? As I see it, I don't have a ring on my finger and no reason to stay in Chicago, and I believe that it's time for me to go. I was trying to hold on and make Chicago work, but it wasn't*

I felt terrible because he was making moves for us, and I was separating us. However, even if there was no man in Louisiana, I realized that he and I would not be together for so many factors. We talked a bit more; we hugged and decided that it was best we did not see each other again.

Now to tell my pastor, one of my closest friends, who is a great inspiration to my daughter and me. This was going to be the hardest. I tried leaving once before, and he begged me not to. He said I was too important to the church, to his family, and others around. This time was different though we cried, prayed, dried our tears, and announced to the church that I was leaving after Sunday Night Live service. He promised that he would never try to stop me from leaving again, nor would he beg me the way that he did previously. Still, I could tell he was saddened. But I think I was a little hurt that he didn't even attempt to stop me. He did say that he felt like the Louisiana guy saw that I wanted desperately to get away and preyed on that.

The day had come for me to make the move to Louisiana. I was super excited! He was driving to Chicago to load all of my things up, and we were driving them back down. He brought a friend with him to assist, and as they were loading items, I left to go and say a few final goodbyes. My girlfriend was in the hospital giving birth to twins; I had to make that trip; I stopped to say goodbye to my mother. Lastly, I went to say my final goodbyes to my pastor! When I got back, they had everything loaded up, and it was time to leave. It was about a 14 hour drive , and I cried almost the entire way.

For the last 32 years, Chicago had been home, and now I was leaving. It felt strange but good! I felt like I was freeing myself from the things I had gotten myself involved in. But in reality,

*You can leave a location and still take the same demons with you.*

I wasn't truly free. I was still putting on a perfected look while still being damaged. But I was off to a new start! I was so happy! I remembered having tears of joy and sadness because I was leaving a place I had known for so long but excited to get started in a new one—a new life, a new career, new surroundings, you name it. I was ready for the newness. Once we got closer to my new home, he said something, and I looked at him strangely. It reminded me of my first husband. I said, wow, he reminds me of him.

I told myself that maybe he reminded me of the good part that I was connected to him, so I ignored the remaining feelings that I was having. Yep, that's it; he reminded me of the good part! We began to unload things as we got home, and family members came over to help us. He said several times *"I would be a fool to cheat on Felicia!"* Once again, I ignored the obvious. It was like he was trying to convince himself that not cheating on me was a good thing. But I did the Felicia thing and ignored what was right before me. He was perfect; well, so I thought. He did everything right, he said the right thing, he was just right! We hung out together, went to all of the football games together, we shared everything. He told me about his ex-girlfriends, flings, and "situations" with his ex-wife. Well, at least the part he wanted me to know.

The time had come, after a couple of days of being there (*remember I said I would not move there unless we were preparing for marriage*), he came in from work, and I was on the computer in the office, and he placed a ring on the desk for me. Yep, you guessed it, that was my big proposal. But I told myself I was happy. It's funny how we tell ourselves that "situations" are ok and we just deal with it.



We started planning for our wedding day. I did not want anything big because most of my friends and family were in Chicago. So we decided to go to Hot Springs, Arkansas, get married outdoors in a beautiful area. We were planning and planning and planning. Then one day he came home from work mad! I could not figure out why he was so angry. This was an attitude and a temper that I had not seen before. But it showed me a side of him that I needed to see, the temper! It was terrible, and I had to do everything in my power to calm him down. What was wrong? He exclaimed, *I'm just tired of her; I'm tired of her, I'm tired of her! Who are you tired of, and why does it make you so upset? It's like she keeps doing everything and all I want to do is be free of her. Who is "her"? The ex-wife! Well, what did she do? I've been trying to get this divorce final, and it's like she's doing everything to stop it.*

Imagine the puzzled look on my face. Maybe it was because I had told myself I was so happy that I did not ask the right questions, or I was furious that he did not tell me that they were still married. I began to think, why didn't my aunt tell me this? I was upset at both of them at this point. The divorce papers have been filed, and we're just waiting on them to be finalized. It takes six months in Louisiana if you have no children and one year if you have kids.

*How long has it been? It's been six months! Our divorce should be final. Why didn't you tell me this? You made it*

The fact of the matter is, now I would be too embarrassed to walk away. This began the disappointment of the situation. It all seems to go downhill from here. Now I'm watching everything, listening to everything, and looking at every move! We decided to go to Hot Springs anyway and have a vacation. We came back after having a great time, just us, and brought back a little puppy in the process.

We ended up waiting two more months before we could get married. But I was here, and so I decided to make the best out of life. He decided he did not want me to work, but I felt like I had to work. After all, I had worked since I was 15 years old. I was going to work. I started substitute teaching at schools in the area. I got a long-term substitute job, and the principal told me I needed to get my degree because I was a natural at teaching. I made up my mind that somehow I was going to get my degree. As the days went on, we moved on through life. People were trying to figure out where I came from, where he got me from, and who I was!

We purchased homes for rental property, and I remember a young lady wanted to rent one of the homes one day. He was upfront and told me this girl he cheated within his first marriage repeatedly. He did not want to go and show her home without my presence or someone else there. I decided to show him I could trust him and said I don't need to be there, it's OK. But he insisted that someone went with him, so my cousin went since I did not want to go. The house was two doors down from our home. He showed her the house as she pulled up with her children and then departed. He and my cousin hung outside for a little bit as I was preparing dinner. I always cook, and everybody was just always over there. I thought it was honorable that he wanted me to see that he was showing this girl the house and wanted me to know that he was trying to be faithful. Hindsight shows he was still trying to convince himself that he could be loyal to me.

So now the divorce is final! We made plans to get married at a City Hall and then have a reception. We went to Arkansas City Hall because he said if we got married in Louisiana, they would post it in the papers, and he did not want his information published for anyone to know anything about him. What he did not want people to know was that he had gotten married so quickly. Nevertheless, I thought I was in love, so I did whatever he suggested. We planned for the reception, people came, and it was a good time. We wanted it to be something small, so we did it at my aunt's school, where she was a principal. He was a part of a Greek organization that typically sings a song during the reception to the wife. It did not happen to me! At the time, I did not know it was supposed to happen until my aunt told me later. Then I began wondering why didn't it happen to me? Was he as into me as he was saying? Or was it a façade? Nevertheless, I am here now!

We began doing life together! We went to church, events, football games, you name it, we did it. This one Sunday, the pastor asked me to preach, and I did. It was an excellent service. The message was anointed and well-received! When we left, he said, I want to preach. I thought it was the most bizarre statement that I had ever heard in my life. The fact is those of us that have been called to preach didn't want to preach, but we do it. But he wanted to preach because he saw the accolades that others gave me. I was kind of furious! I did not know if I was mad at him or mad at God. God knew I did not want to date or be around another preacher, and now he is saying God called him to preach. I didn't believe God called him. He liked the fame that came with preaching. Nevertheless, I did the Felicia thing, and I supported my husband. If he was going to preach, he had to know what he was saying. We joined a church where my cousin was the pastor, and he ordained both of us. I was ordained before in the COGIC organization as an evangelist, and he was never ordained. So he decided to ordain both of us under the Baptist organization.

He preached his licensing sermon, which I wrote for him. We continued attending the church, helping and working wherever help was needed. Somewhere during that time, my cousin stepped down, and they were without a Pastor. This means the church was now looking for someone. The church met with the preaching staff and said they wanted to look at all of us as possible future pastors. I did not want to be included in that number for several reasons.

1). I did not believe that the Baptist organization would ever accept a female pastor.

2). I did not want the competition between my husband and myself.

3). I knew the calling on my life and how I ministered.

I also knew that I was not assigned to lead there. So I agreed to step out of the running and take on teaching Bible class because none of the men wanted that task. This allowed them all to be in the rotation to be considered as the next pastor. As it got time for voting, they eventually voted him in as pastor. Every service that he had to preach for his Sunday in the rotations, his sermons were written by me. If I did not write them, he would start them, and I would go in and tweak them to make them great. After all, I preached for 15 years, and knowing how to put a sermon together comes with time. But he was not the kind of preacher that I was used to. All the preachers around me were powerful preachers; they knew what to say and when to say it. He was a great teacher but not the greatest preacher. I used to wish he would just find his way and do it the way that was comfortable for him. But he wanted to do it the way everybody else was doing it; he wanted to be that kind of preacher.

Then the unthinkable happened. If I remember correctly, things started to change after day number 364 of being married before the 2nd year began. He was coming home extremely late. He no longer included me in decisions. He was doing many of the activities we used to do together but now without me. I was making a note in my mental memory bank, and it did not feel good. I remember thinking what a fool I am! I left everything I knew to be with this man to treat me this way. One day, I was working on the computer, and I got an inbox message on Facebook that said, *"you don't know me, but I've seen you. Remember the day that a lady came to look at the house two doors down from you? That was me. I just want you to know that your husband and I have been having an affair. I slept with him throughout his first marriage and now several times since you and he have been together."* My heart sank. I began crying and screaming. I could not believe this was happening, but I knew she was not lying. I had felt it for a while. I just did not know who, where, or when. She said, *"one of the new houses you all just purchased we met there to show me the house. In times in the past, this was our thing and how we would hook up. He would pretend like he wanted to show me the place to rent and never rented it to me, but we would meet there and have sex".* When I confronted him, of course, he lied and said she was not telling the truth. But she was able to describe this house that he and I had just purchased perfectly.. If it were something in the past, she would not know anything about this particular house. And it was a different house from the one-two doors down from us. Once again, I swallowed my pride and stayed there because I would be too embarrassed to walk away. Some situations we get ourselves into forces us to be someone we don't want to and you cannot even face looking in the mirror. But he promised from this moment on he would be faithful to only me. I remember thinking back to things that I had done in my past and being with someone else's husband before. Maybe this was my "reap what you sow" moment. At least that's what I told myself, I was getting back what I had dished out, so who was I not to forgive him.

I forgave him! However, it did not end there. It was the beginning of things getting worse. I knew there were others, but I had no proof. I told myself that God would show me exactly what I needed to see, And He did! There was one person that was a member of our church and had a high position in the church. I knew we were not friends, but she was someone that I was extremely cordial with. She used to walk up to me and hug me every Sunday, and now all of a sudden, every time she saw me, she would walk in the other direction. The church was not that big, so to make a considerable effort to go all the way on the other side of the church to avoid me said something. I would not say anything; I would just watch. But I was very hurt and mad, not necessarily at her, but at him because she owed me nothing.

He confided in someone who told him that he needs to make the next portion of your life be all about having a healthy marriage. This person reminded him that people will come into your life and ruin your marriage and ministry. You will be stuck while they are in the middle of it all, making you look bad. Grow your church, build it with your wife and leave all else alone! He told me all of this after a church service, while we were at dinner. He said that he would leave everybody else alone, and take their advice. He said, *"the devil is terrified of us and will send people in our lives to distract us. I want to only focus on you and me"*. I was thinking, It all sounded great but I knew it would not happen in reality.

Life continued, and he began to disappear more and more. He started having more out-of-town trips "for work." I'll never forget it was around Christmas 2012, and he was going to a soccer tournament for his school. It was a double hitter, so he decided to stay away instead of coming home. I knew that this was wrong and all a lie. He did not go to the at home soccer games, so why was he going to the away soccer games? I called because I said I'm going to meet you there. He initially said he would call once he got there to give the address. But he never called so I called him and he never answered the phone. I rushed home from work to pack because I was going to where he was. However, I sat at home for hours, waiting for him to answer the phone or call me with the location. The next day he called me saying he was on his way home. He told me that it was a double game that went into triple over-time in the last game, so it was so late that he decided to stay in that area. The soccer team wasn't the best, so to go into a triple hitter was a stretch. I hated arguing, but more so, I didn't want to let him know I was starting to figure things out. I was building my case.

He asked me for my sizes because he planned to stop at the store and buy some things. This was an enormous red flag. He never shops! I purchased everything for the both of us, from socks to clothes. I bought everything. He didn't even know his size. But the God in me said to be quiet, give him your sizes and let's see what this will be. When he came home, he had some gifts for me; a couple of shirts, perfume or something of that nature. I don't remember it being anything that I would love. But I told myself he was trying. I then said, what did you buy yourself because you did not just stop in the store to buy some-thing for me? I knew that once he showed me the items "he had for himself," that they were all purchased by someone else. They consisted of cologne sets, sweaters, watches, and gym shoes. I was livid. They were all Christmas gifts given to him by another female. I let it be known that I knew exactly what they were. But he told me I was crazy, trippin, and losing control! I started thinking, "am I losing control? Am I tripping? Am I crazy?" I apologized to him and said, I am going to stop believing the worst.

I prepared for bed and noticed that my daughter had absolutely everything on in her room. The lights were on, the iPad was on, the iPod was going, her phone was lit up, and she was sleeping. I went into the room to turn some of her gadgets off and noticed she had several messages on her iPad. This was the interesting thing: everyone in the house used my iTunes account. He used it on his phone to download the same music I had; she used it so I could watch her activities and make sure she was doing things age-appropriate. So when I got ready to turn the iPad off, somehow, when everybody was connected to the internet, the messages were intercepted and sent to her iPad. She was getting all of his text messages. The last text read "sitting at home having a cocktail without my baby is making me sad." I wrote down the number and entered that number into my cell phone to see if I had that contact saved. Wouldn't you know it, it was the girl from the church. I read through all of the messages. They had spent an entire weekend together when he was supposedly on an away trip for school. I said to him, you made me think I was crazy, and I prayed and asked God to relieve me and whatever I needed to see reveal it. He worked fast and allowed me to see it. I said, *"I'm leaving! I was done! I'm sick of you. You irritate me; I cannot believe you had me move down here and give up my life for you to treat me this way."* My exact words were, *"you are a piece of shit!"*

The following day reality hit, where was I going to go? I knew it was time for me to start getting things in order because it was only a matter of time before I would be leaving for good. Several other incidents had taken place, and of course, by now, they saw each other regularly. He would visit her at her house quite often. One day, iPhone came out with a new update where it showed you the locations of your iPhone. Since all iPhones and gadgets were under my iTunes account, my iPhone info was everybody's iPhones. I did not know what it was because it was new, so I clicked on it, and it said his iPhone and the location. I knew her address, so I did a screenshot and sent it to him and said, unless you want this to go out to all of the deacons at the church, you better leave her house and leave now. She lived about 20 minutes away, and he was home in five minutes.

I have no idea how he got home so quickly, but he hurried up and got home. He was trying to convince me that she had called him for prayer. I could not take it! I cannot make this stuff up; somebody is going to think I'm crazy for real. It sounds like a movie, and I'm being punked in the movie. We got no sleep that night. We argued all night. I was perplexed about how the man with erectile dysfunction could sleep around as much as he was sleeping around. How are you taking Cialis that does not work for us but yet you're having multiple affairs? What I knew was that my heart could not take anymore and I was pretty much done with the marriage. I just did not know when I was going to have a clear way of escape. I endured until I could not endure anymore. I had tapped out of the marriage so much that I did not care what he did, where he went, and who he was with. I made up my mind; I would do to him what he had done to me. I even told him not to take my kindness for weakness. I am saved because I want to be, not because I have to be. I had connected with someone else, but I was discreet. It didn't last long because I was only connecting with others to hurt him as he hurt me, but I couldn't afford to ruin my reputation.

He came in one day and told me that he had sold one of the rental properties, and the closing date was the very next day. Wow! You must've been working on this for a very long time. He said, "No, an investor approached me and said they had cash so that we could get around the red tape. But the title company said you have to come in and sign a document since you're my wife. *Can you do that tomorrow at about noon?" "What time will you be going? Can I just go with you?" "Oh, I can't get there until later, and I'm not sure what time that will be, so go ahead and you just sign at 12."*

I went there the next day, signed the paperwork, and prepared to leave. The title company said, *"what time will your husband and your church member be here to sign their documents?"* I replied, *"And my who?"* I left the building and called him and said, *you're selling this house to your mistress? I knew that if I had told you, you would have acted like this, so this is why I did not say anything! That's fine,* and I hung up the phone. I made a U-turn in the street, went back to the title company, and said, *hey, I do this for a living; I should have read those documents. May I have a look at those documents to see what I signed?* She handed me the originals and said, you can go in this office over here and read them. I tore them up in little bitty pieces and left.

I then said, *"if they have any issues, have them give me a call."* I walked out saying that you won't make a business deal with your mistress and keep me in the dark, not on my watch. This was not a cash deal as he had said; she had gotten financed for it. He did not think he would need my signature, but we lived in a community property state. As long as we were married, everything he owned belonged to me as well. The deal was that he would walk away with about $75,000 from the house sale, and it was her birthday weekend. When I began to connect the dots, he had been planning this for a while. He was preparing to go out of town for the weekend, all I kept thinking was not on my watch.

I got home that day, and I knew this was the last day that I would be with him. I drove around until I found an apartment. So many of the apartments had a waiting list. I drove past these condominium apartments, and there was a sign out that said it was for rent. I called and made an appointment to view it the same day. I went and looked at it, and it was the cutest tiny apartment ever, and it was going to work for my daughter and me. With no hesitation, I signed the lease and gave her security and the first month's rent. I went home and got something to sleep in and stayed there alone. I made arrangements for my daughter to go to one of her friend's house, and I slept in the apartment on the floor that night by myself. I remember praying and crying all night long.

The next day I went back to the house to get all of my things. He swore there's no way I found an apartment that fast and that I had this in the plan all along. The truth is, I was no longer going to argue. I had been doing that for years, and all I wanted now was my freedom to start over. It took me two trips to get everything out of his house. Once I got everything out, I had to come back the next day to tighten up some loose ends. When I got there, he was not home and had not been home all night, but his car was there, and his guns were missing. He left me a note that looked like a suicide note. I called the police, and I called his mother. When the police read the note, they too stated it sounded like a suicide note. After being there for about an hour, he walked through the door. They took him in for an evaluation. He was pretty popular in our town, so he was able to get out the same day. Usually, you have to stay for three days. But he wasn't my concern any longer. The only time he reached out to me was to sign the documents for the house to be sold. I finally gave in and said I don't care. It's not my house; I'll sign the paperwork. I went there to go and sign the paperwork, and low and behold, the mistress was there too.

She said to me, *what are you looking at?* I remember being on the phone with someone. I put my car in park because I had it. *"Girl, you better shut up talking to me"* is all I remember saying.

*"You don't tell me to shut up, this makes no sense. You could've just signed those papers." "And you could have just found your own man, but you are the classic preacher's whore."*

I cannot remember what else I said, but I know I called her everything but a child of God. I also remember calling her a moose face and that nobody would ever want her. Her exact words were, *"your husband wants me; in fact, he wanted all of this, and when you're kissing him, you're kissing my pussy."* I got ready to get out of the car because I knew at that moment I was about to go to jail for whipping her @$$. I believe I was on the phone with my god kid's mother, and she said don't do it, stay in the car, do not get out. It was as if God himself was talking to me. I did not go in to sign the papers, and I just pulled off and left.

I decided to continue with my life and a new direction. I continued going to the church for about 2 to 3 Sundays because I had told myself that the church members did not deserve what we were going through, and they had become accustomed to me being there. But I remember the very last Sunday that I attended. It was around my birthday, and he usually sings a birthday song to all of the members. This one particular Sunday, he made a big deal about my birthday and how much "he still loved me" as if I was the one that had wronged him. I was in utter disbelief. I was furious and almost went into a rage. The rest of the service was a blur; I was trying to figure out how to make my exit. I used to keep my tambourine up under my chair. I remember grabbing it sitting it on my lap because I knew this was my last Sunday, and the minute the benediction was over, I left out the side door, never to return.

I started having Monday night prayers in my home with a few preacher wives and a couple of others. This was my way of giving back to others and building up what I know God has placed on the inside. I also had a group of young adults that would come over, and we would get together and shed. We would just sing all night. It had become therapy for me. I remember posting a couple of videos on Facebook of us singing. I got a call that said:

*"You're embarrassing me. What are you talking about? You are doing all of this, hanging out, going places, and posting them to let people see that we aren't together.*

*How narcissistic was that?"*

I was appalled that he could even call me and say that. What in the world was going on, and how do you turn this around on me?

I was trying to rebuild my life and come up with my next plan. I remember Doritos does a contest every year for whoever comes up with the best Super Bowl commercial would win $1 million. I had come up with a wonderful commercial and got a lot of people involved. We filmed it and posted it on Facebook. The entire town went crazy over it. Then, my soon-to-be-ex, called me saying we should get back together. The one thing about him is he's motivated by money and the thought of me possibly winning $1 million; he did not want to be on the losing end of that. Plus, everyone in the town was saying how good the commercial was. I did not win the commercial, and the request died down for us to get back together.

My lease was only for six months because I did not know if I was gone for good or if we would work things out. But at the end of that six months, I knew there was no way that I was ever going back. I found a bigger home to rent and moved there.

Now I had to build new ministry circles. This is where I found out that being in the south and being a female minister was much harder than it was for men. Had I been a male going through a divorce, no one would care, but many had isolated me. Those asking me to preach regularly weren't even speaking to me, But it was OK because those with whom I had built an alliance were his people. So I got invited to preach because I was his wife, and once I was getting a divorce, those invites dried up. The fact of the matter is I was known throughout the town as his wife, and most people did not even know my first name. So I started attending other services. He called me again to say I was embarrassing him. I I asked him, how am I embarrassing him now?

*"By going to all of these services hanging out in public." "So you mean to tell me you expect me to just sit in the house and do absolutely nothing? I did that for five years, thinking if I stayed home, that you would stay home and not cheat or that I could see if you were doing anything. That got me nowhere! I will never do that again; there's no way that I will sit around and lose my life because you're not comfortable." "You are going to keep on, and something is going to happen to you. What? Are you threatening me now? Let me get off this phone. I need to call the police and make sure that they are aware of this. You're gonna mess around, and your body is going to be cut up in little bitty parts, and no one will be able to find you. What?*

It was at that moment I realized his ex-wife was not lying. I was told she said he would do this kind of stuff for real. Allegedly, he had threatened her at gunpoint. I hung up the phone. Two seconds later, I received a text message from him, *are you OK? I just wanted to make sure that you were OK. Hadn't talked to you today.* I do not know who or what I was dealing with. He called and said one thing and then text and said another. He was trying to cover his tracks so that if I called the police, he would say that was the only time he reached out to me. I just cut the communication, and the next time I talked to him, we signed divorce papers.

The day I went before the judge to get the divorce signed off, I remember thinking I'm finally about to be free. When I got before the judge, I noticed it was his fraternity brother. He read the paperwork and said, hold on; one moment, went back into his chambers and came back out, saying, *"I'm going to have to give you a continuation because something isn't right with your paperwork."* I was so furious because I knew he went into that office and called him and asked him if he knew I was there getting a divorce. Because the minute I walked out of the courtroom, he was calling me saying, *"oh, you're trying to get a divorce."* I didn't even understand the statement because we had signed the divorce papers before the notary; it was only a matter of time before the divorce was final. Since we weren't asking for anything and had no kids, it was OK to move forward. Nevertheless, I had to wait another 30 days, and God knows I was not happy.

During this time, I had preached at a service, and someone said the Lord told them to sow into my life. They wrote a check for $2000. I will never forget how excited I was because God knew I needed the money. I remembered calling my mother, saying, look what happened. I was just praying about money, and now I was given this amount. Well, to my surprise, the next day that same person came to my job and sat in my office and asked me out for a date. I said, *"what? I'm still married, and you are married, and I'm not doing that."* He had a very perplexed look on his face as if I was supposed to go on this date with him because he had just given me this money. I said I couldn't be bought, and you said God told you to give me that. He left out saying, *"You're gonna be my girlfriend."* I laughed and walked away. I remember seeing him at a Walgreens; we were driving the same type of car. It was like that made him mad! But I could not let it bother me; I was already dealing with a lot. The next day I got a call from the manager saying she was coming over to meet with me. She had tears in her eyes as she connected me on a call with a security team. I have never been in trouble, so I'm like, *"what is this?"* The man had gone to another branch and told them I asked him for money, he gave it to me as a loan, and I refused to give it back. That was a big company, and it was unethical to borrow money from customers or even make gifts over $25. Since it was given to me at the church, I didn't consider it a bank issue. Nevertheless, it got me terminated from a job. What in the world was I going to do now? I remember the scripture that stated,

*"Give her the fruit of her hands; And let her works praise her in the gates." Proverbs 31:31*

The one thing I knew was the ability to cook in my hands, and everyone loved my cooking. I started Wangs-N-Thangz. Everyone loves my wings. I cooked them right out of my home and began to sell plates. It sustained me! During lunchtime, I had a line outside of my door every day. Well, here it goes again; he heard about it and said we should not get a divorce; we should open your chicken business in my building because everybody is saying it's a gold mine! Once again, narcissism rises to an all-time high. Nope, I'm not going to do it.

I continue to move on with life, so I also got a part-time seasonal job at Lowe's. I absolutely hated this job, but I did it with a smile every day! So much so, that after two weeks of working there, they promoted me to supervisor. But that still was not enough to pay my bills. I remember crying at night, working there, telling God this is not what you promised me, and I remember telling him what he did promise me. Within one week, the corporate office called me and offered me a management position in sales. I did not get the job at the store that I was working at but at another store 30 minutes away. I thought it's perfect! I'll move to that area!

Finally, the 30 days were up, and I was divorced, and as this situation was ending, I was starting a new me. Well, creating a new me, I remember thinking, what was I going to do differently?

*If we don't ask ourselves the hard questions, we will do the same thing again.*

But we cannot just ask ourselves those questions; we have to take what we've learned or what we find out and apply it daily.

Oh well, off to a new situation!

**Journal Entry:**

- Can you identify some unhealthy patterns you may have adopted when entering a relationship? Are you choosing the same type of people?
- Are you asking the right questions?
- Find a Bible verse that encourages you and meditate on it for the rest of this week.

# SITUATION 5

*TRYING SOMETHING NEW*

I am now 46 years old. I have got to figure out this thing called life. Why do I continue to make the same mistakes over and over again? I'm now in a new area, Ruston, Louisiana, a new house and a new job. Maybe this is it! The sad part is that once again, I left the area that I was in, I thought it would give me a new start.

> *Unless you do the work and change within yourself, the new beginning does not happen. You have just taken your old self and placed it in a new area. You still have the same habits, the same issues and the same disappointments; just in a different location.*

Things with the job were going well, and I was ready to start dating again. The problem is I didn't hang out other than church. I did not want a churchy man. I wanted someone that loved God, went to church and enjoyed life. I decided to join a dating app. I really wanted someone different than what I had ever experienced before. I met a man of another race, and I thought this must be God. For several reasons: 1). I wanted a multiracial church. And a black and white couple would help with that. 2). I had never dated a white man before. Maybe this is my "do something different". 3). He loved God but was not "churchy."

I met him in March 2015. He lived in Jackson and I in Ruston, an almost 2-hour difference in our drive. On our first day, we met at a place for crawfish in the Jackson area. He was handsome, suave, and a smooth talker. I enjoyed hanging with him. We loved easy and fast. The one thing this relationship taught me was balance. Fact is, I had been in church all of my life and was a homebody. He brought me out of being a homebody and being able to have a balanced life. So I enjoyed the outside world for the first time in my life since I was young. But then the arguments started. I never remember what the arguments were about. They all seemed foolish when we were done. I absolutely hate arguments, so I try to end them most times by just apologizing quickly. But the next day, he would rehash the same argument, and it would last for three and four days. I said I'm not going to be able to do this relationship. When he was sober, he would always apologize until he got drunk again, then we repeated the same argument. But we continued dating.

We talked about marriage, but I knew we were not ready. The talk was only to see if we were on the same page, or so I thought. But we had some fantastic times. Not every day was full of arguments. We had terrific hangouts. He went with me to my family reunion and met all of my family, and then eventually started going to church with me.

I remember the Sunday morning he walked into church with me. Sunday school was still going on, so we eased in and sat in the back. As soon as the door opened a couple of the members turned around and looked at us and then did a double-take because I had never brought anyone to church with me. He enjoyed church, and he continued to come every Sunday. We hung out with my Bishop and his wife after church, going to eat on Sunday. Things were good until they were not.

Two months into our relationship, it's now May 2015 and my Bishop was having an all-white birthday party. We decided to go, and we had a great time, good food, dancing, and a grand celebration. There seemed to be a lot of whispering around me, and I was oblivious to it. But I was having a great time just enjoying the day and the ambiance. The decorations were beautiful, the food was terrific, and the group of people were great. The time came for everyone to get up to give words of thanks to our Bishop for the celebration of his birthday. Then they called my guy up to also give words. I was looking weird because he did not know him that long. Why was he being called up? Oh well, go with the flow Felicia! He later gives this long speech about when he met me, how we met, and how much in love with me he was. I was still looking like this is Bishop's birthday; why are you talking about me? As he continued to speak, I realized, oh my God, he is about to propose. We were not ready today. I knew that one day I would want to be with him or marry him, but today we were not ready.

The crowd was happy and cheering. This church celebrated marriage! Those that were married loved marriage, those that were not were desiring to be married. I remember him proposing, and I looked at him as he put the ring on my finger, and I hugged him and whispered, I'm accepting this because we are in front of so many people, but we are not ready to get married and will not even discuss a date until at least a year from now. He said OK. Although we were not ready, I was still happy!

The following Sunday, the video was played throughout the church; everybody that was not there was excited and saying congratulations. I posted the video on Facebook, and everybody loved it and was crying. There were still so many that were not happy. I had some family members and close friends that do not believe in mixed marriages that were not as happy. But this was my life, and I get to live it. I wanted something different, and maybe this would be the thing that I would be able to prove to myself that I could make a marriage work. I knew that I was one of those people who grew up believing that I was called to be a wife. My best friend always said, you know how to be a wife! In fact, you know how to be a darn good wife. You give until you can't give anymore! The problem is you don't pick suitable husbands.

As sure as you know it, the arguments rekindled. This time we were hitting below the belt; we were both saying ugly and mean things. I believe I thought that the things that I forgave in other relationships, I was not willing to be as forgiving because he was white. Ouch! I saw, for the first time, myself being prejudiced. Why would I not extend the same grace to him that I would extend to others I had been in a relationship with simply because of the skin color difference. I realized then that sometimes the same thing we accuse others of doing we find ourselves doing as well. I found myself being prejudiced towards him by not extending the same grace I would give to someone else simply because the color of his skin was different.

Oh, but the arguments intensified! This time we had to get my Bishop involved. He decided to counsel us, and I'm sure he thought it would be a simple session. I did not say much, although I did share my concerns. But he shared a lot, and it was almost like he was arguing all over again. We left that session still with unresolved issues and realizing that we will agree to disagree. Later that night, the argument started up again after he was drinking. I remember crying hard, saying to myself, there's no way I could do this. He went on to say, keep the engagement ring, sell it, pay off some of your bills because I'm done, I won't be back.

That night he left, and he called attempting to apologize the following day, but I was done! There was no way I could be in a relationship like this. It was too toxic and too much for me to deal with at this age and stage of my life. When I said that to him, he started cursing me out more and more. It did not matter; I was done. But this was hard for me and good at the same time. The hard part was figuring out what this insertion of my life was for. Why did God allow this? What was the entire big proposal for? More importantly, why did I love so fast? But the good part was this time; I did not continue as I did in the past when I saw that something was wrong. So instead of looking at the glass as half empty, I said it's half full. Maybe the lesson was to show me after going through the first four situations; now, I am at situation five, I finally got it. It's OK to walk away. It's OK not to be OK! And it's OK to deal with the embarrassment behind a decision you chose to make and then pull away from it because it's not right.

I went on Facebook, and I made a big post. The post stated: "*many of you walked with me through my recent proposal and were excited about the proposal. Thank you for sharing your excitement with me about the next stage of my life. However, I am writing this to say I have decided to call off my engagement. I know many of you would say you don't owe us this explanation; however, I feel that I invited you into what I thought was happiness for me; it's only right that I invite you into the closure of that part of my life. The relationship was so toxic and I had to walk away. No one deserves to argue every day and deal with what I have dealt with over the last couple of months. Once again, thank you for sharing in the excitement; please pray for me during this time.*"

Maybe I finally got it!

**Journal Entry:**

- Starting today, how can you do things differently?
- Identify some of your bad habits or behavior. Once you identify them, it can help to choose something different.
- List your most recent Ah Ha moment, when you realized you finally got it.

# SITUATION 6



*ROLLER COASTER*

As I stand in this big empty building of what used to be a completely filled church I am in awe. How did we get here? How did it get to this point? What happened? I wish I had the answers to those questions but it still seems so puzzling and hurtful. I once thought we could conquer the world together, but now I stand solo trying to figure out my next. How could the man who once loved me take everything that I worked so hard for? With all that happened I knew it was the time to either close the church or shut down for a period and reconvene at a later date. I got the call from a member that was showing the church to someone who wanted to sublease it and purchase all of the items inside. The call was in a frantic *"Pastor everything is gone, there is nothing here!" What? There's no way I was just there yesterday and this was a church building full of furniture equipment and everything. Call the police. I know he took it, we will let them and the insurance figure it out.*

But what actually got us here? This is where it looks like a complete roller coaster. That's what I call this situation. A situation that began tremendously and slowly grew worse and got out of hand because I did not deal with the issues that had caused it to spread in the first place.

I was living in Ruston, Louisiana. My goddaughter had decided she would find my next person to date because, according to her, I was not choosing good quality men for myself. I thought she would choose one of her college professors; instead, she went to an online dating site. She would sit at my house and ask if someone asked you this question, how would you respond. After so many of those questions, I wondered what she was doing? She then told me she had signed me up for an online dating site and she was communicating with a couple of people, one in particular that she liked a lot for me. I told her to give me the computer, the username, and the password. The reason being, there's no way a 24-year-old could respond the way a 45-year-old would respond even if I were telling her the answers. I continued and talked to a couple of the people that she was communicating with. There were two, in particular, that had my attention.

I went on dates with both of them, and there was something about both that I liked and something I disliked. I knew I was looking for something different. I just did not know how different. One was a total street guy, and the other was quite nerdy. I hung out with the street guy a few times, and it was different. It felt like if I pursued him, I would be returning to the lifestyle I had escaped. I knew I wouldn't be able to hang with him for long. He was just something to do. I then went on a date with the nerdy guy. I was very sure I did not like him! He didn't dress the way I like; his conversation was about him and what he does with little about me. We made plans for a second and third date, and I canceled both of them. The signs were there; why didn't I pay attention? But he asked again, and I told myself if you want something different, you have to do something different. So, I went on an official second date with him and decided he was not that bad. Still nerdy! But not bad.

We decided to make it official; however, there were still so many other women he was talking to. We lived one hour and 45 minutes apart, so when we made plans, it had to cover many hours to make the drive worth it. I'll never forget the day I came to spend my days off with him. I went on a <u>Tuesday evening</u> and was supposed to leave early <u>Thursday morning</u> to be at work. I decided to call off that

Thursday and spend one more day. Little to my surprise, he had made plans for that day. As usual, he went to work, came home, and we decided to go out to eat. As we were driving back, he stated, "hey, remember that girl that I told you that calls me all day and night?"

*Yeah why what's up? I think she's following us.*

I was looking at something on my phone and never lifted my head. However, I remember being on what felt like a high-speed chase. For miles, she chased us, and he drove to a casino and parked; she blocked us in. He jumped out of the car, telling her to move. She was yelling, *"I am not moving, I am not moving! She needs to know that you and I had plans today." "Move girl; I don't have any plans with you; move your car!" "I'm not moving anywhere."* She stood there and kept him from closing his door. *Did you tell her you were just with me?* He leaned his head in the car and said, "call the police." She rushes over to my door, banging on the window. I let the window down. *"Did he tell you that me and him are messing around? Whatever is going on is between you and him; please walk away from this side of the door."*

She gave me this strange look like what kind of woman would not want to know, but I continued to look unbothered. Still having us blocked, and he yells, just call the police again. I reach for my phone, and as she's heading back to her car, she makes the statement, "make sure you tell her that you were just at my house performing sexual favors." I still showed no expression, but I was agitated because what she stated made sense to me. The week prior, he made a pop-up visit to my home. I live an hour and 45 minutes away; you don't just pop up. But he said he wanted to surprise me, so I went with it, again ignoring the obvious signs that something wasn't right. I was excited to see him, though. Getting to know him later, those types of surprises are not in him to do! I should have known something.

There was nothing but silence in that car on the drive back to his house. I immediately start getting my bag and things to leave. He came into the room and begged me not to go. *"I will end all communication with her; I promise, just don't leave me."* I told him then there were two things I would not deal with again in any relationship: infidelity and abuse. When I questioned what she meant by he was just at her home, he stated she called him to borrow $60, and he drove it to her, and then since he was so close, he decided to stop and see me. I let it go because I hate going back and forth, but I should have dug deeper. Who needs to borrow money and you have to bring it to them too. Her story made more sense. She needed the money, but to get it, she had to engage in activities. I let it go, but I was watchful.

Things continued and were going great! We had a birthday cele-bration and hung out with friends. You name it, we did it! We were enjoying each other's company and getting to know each other. Within three months of our relationship, we traveled out of town to meet his family. I didn't know that he had already told his family that he knew I was "the one." I was feeling the same way! He was attentive, loving, very supportive, and seemed to have had my back. He appeared to be everything that I have never had before. Could this be what I have been missing all along?

After meeting his family and returning home on one of our walks, he stated he wanted me to move with him. I said I need a job to make that kind of move. Why would you need a job? I can take care of every-thing? I knew I would not feel right unless I could have my own money, even if he would take care of everything. I asked, so if I got a job are you looking for me to get an apartment close by? Why would you do that? No, just move with me, he said. But I began looking for a job and finally got an offer. In the middle of December that year, I transitioned and moved to Mississippi. Immediately things got strange.

I have never lived with anyone before marriage, and I began feeling trapped. He started reaching out to some old loves. One happened to be the girl who chased us around, one who lived far away and his daughter's mom. After looking at his phone one day, I realized the same I love you messages he was sending me he was also sending them. Once again, I felt like such a fool! I had given up my home, giving up my job once again for what I thought was love. I was sad a lot! And it was this way for a while. He started keeping his phone on silent, added a lock code and the phone was always faced down so that the screen was not visible.

As we approached Christmas, he told me that he goes out of town to spend time with his kids for two weeks during the Christmas break and stays at his and his ex-wife's home with her. I started agreeing with things I would not usually have because I had just moved here. How do I tell everyone now that, oops, I made a big mistake?

While he was out of town, my goddaughter came to visit me. I began sharing with her some of my concerns. She said to me, well, I wasn't going to tell you, but you remember after your birthday gathering in Ruston when I went outside to move my car, he made the statement, *"you have my number, call me sometime"*. She said I looked puzzled like what; And continued moving the vehicle. She said, but he called me since he has been out of town, and I missed the call and called him back. I did not know if I should be furious with him or with her. I should be furious with him! How dare you approach someone in my circle? With her, how dare you not tell me this at the time it happened? That could have changed a lot. I am more than sure I never would have made that move with that piece of information being shared.

Once again, I dummied it down and did not deal with the obvious because I did not want to look foolish because I had now found myself in another "situation" that I should never have been in. I continued on in the relationship as usual. We decided to move into an apartment that was ours and not one that he already had. By now, my 16-year-old daughter is coming back from Chicago. It was summertime; his boys were there for their break as well. Everyone played video games all day and night; in fact, I was the oddball. But that's what they did, and everyone was together. Our lives continued, the boys went back home after summer vacation, and my daughter went back to Chicago for school.

For a while, It was just us, and we were living our peaceful lives. I thought it was very peaceful, but I had agreed to something that was never what I wanted for my life. Things like, no girl's trips and we had to go everywhere and do everything together. But he was so attentive, so it just made sense. He seemed like the perfect man! The thing that I was missing, I now seemed to have. The one thing he did not have was the spiritual side, and I had told myself I did not need that in him, and I was tired of church men. Little did I know, that was going to be a problem later!

It was birthday time again, his birthday was first, and I had planned something every week leading up to his birthday. Since that's the way I like to celebrate my birthday, it was only fitting that I do the same for him. The big birthday gift that year for him was to take him to a live Dallas Cowboys game. He loved that team and had never been to a live game. It was a fantastic time we had. It was time for my birthday the next month, and absolutely nothing was planned. As it came to a couple of days before, I was asked what do you want to do? I was not happy, but I did not say I was not pleased. We went out to dinner at a local restaurant, and as we were eating. He placed an engagement ring on the table and continued eating. That was my big proposal. It was not the type of proposal I was looking for, but it was a proposal. I thought to myself, I no longer had to live in sin and shacking. He also purchased a car for me since I had lost my car, so I did not make a big deal about the lack of planning for my birthday.

As I reflect, I realize that I never got gifts on Valentine's Day, Mother's Day, birthday, or Christmas, but I was constantly flooding him with gifts. For some reason, I would not share what mattered to me with him. I would just continue as if those days meant nothing to me. Our lives became very boring. We did not go anywhere except to our daily run to Walmart, maybe a walk in the park or the gym to work out. But again, I had told myself I never had that before. Usually, those are things that I did alone, and finally, I had someone who enjoyed those things.

We planned our wedding for April the following year. We decided to get married in his hometown, and his mom would perform the ceremony. Things seemed strange surrounding our wedding, in terms of what we could share on social media or invitations being sent out. I hadn't realized that we were being secretive. Nevertheless, I continued with our plans. It was almost time to get married, April had finally arrived! Before that, it was my daughter's sweet 16, so of course, we had to go all-out with a big party, DJ, food, you name it we had it. She was given a promise ring from my soon to be husband that she would wait until marriage before engaging in sexual activities.

After that was over, it was immediately time for our wedding, so we flew to New Jersey to get married. We had to get there a few days early to get the marriage license. We hung out with family, went to church, and ate well before the actual ceremony. I remember sitting on the bed at his sister's house, and the ex-wife had called and asked what he was doing. He said, oh, I'm just sitting on the bed watching TV. True enough, that is what we were doing, but we were not at home, and we were about to get married, which was not mentioned. I wondered why but I never addressed it.

Everyone was being secretive about us getting married, but why? Even more than why, why didn't I ask? Why did I ignore this?

Nevertheless Everyone arrived in town, and we got married! One of the things that he loved about me is that I did not question a lot. Ironically, that's what I hated most. I didn't ask the right questions. My lack of questioning made him feel like I was on "his team." Those were the words he constantly used, and I heard them throughout the marriage. I heard it so much that I became that. I did everything he wanted me to do, and the things I wanted to do were never done. I found myself lonely and never sharing it, not happy and not talking about it, and very dissatisfied sexually. I would not discuss any of my frustrations. When I would bring up my concerns about our marriage, I was shut down and made to feel like I could not talk about what was on my heart without feeling like it was my fault. I was blamed for things all of the time, and things were turned around to make it seem like everything was all my fault. I constantly heard you forced yourself to move here; you forced us into getting married; I do everything for you, you don't do anything! So hearing those things, I felt like I could not share what I was feeling without being blamed.

We are now back home, living our married lives and trying to figure ourselves out. It's time for the summer which means the kids are coming with us for the summer. I never minded because his kids were some of the sweetest kids ever. All they wanted to do was play video games, and they did not bother anyone! My daughter also came home, and this time she stayed and went to school with us. She was the typical teenager that was trying to find herself. She began doing things, lying on people a lot and just acting out overall. One day she was being punished, and all of her gadgets were being taken. We were going back-and-forth. She said, *"that's why I stay in my room all the time, and now you want to take the door off the hinges, but I can't stand being out in the open."*

*What are you talking about?* She got quiet. My goddaughters were there, and we decided to go to the store to take a ride to see if we could get her to talk. What is going on with you? I kept asking her over and over. Finally, she broke her silence; *I'm tired; you have no idea what's going on with me, fine, I will tell you exactly what it is.*

We were sitting in the car outside the apartment, and she yelled *Your husband asked me for sex. What are you talking about? That's why I've been staying in my room and not coming out, and you keep asking what's wrong. Even when I get out of the shower, I feel like he's always looking at me, so I run and make a mad dash for my room.* I was really in disbelief. I could not believe that she was saying this about the man that I had just married. She had just got caught lying about my ex-husband and some other people, so I could not believe her.

I thought she's always saying things when she gets in trouble to save herself or make herself look great. It was rough! She said, fine, I'll prove it to you. She ran into the house when we got back to the apartment, ran up the stairs, and yelled, *"it's all out; my mom knows everything, I told her everything, and you can take this ring you gave me and shove it. I am done. I made sure she knew everything! Shut the F*CK up, get the F*CK out of here."* I was torn. Do I believe my daughter, which I usually would but she was just caught in a bunch of lies about other people doing the same. Who do I believe, this man I just married who had never shown me any sign of this type of action, or my daughter?

The next couple of months were very rough. I was so far removed from the marriage, having crazy thoughts: Is this true or not true. It was about Christmas time, and we had all decided to go and visit my oldest daughter in Atlanta. His exact words were, I'm not going because I don't know what's been said, and everybody will be looking at me crazy. In hindsight, when I look back on that, he never denied what she said; he just said he was offended that she thought he would hurt her. I would never do anything to hurt that girl. I can't believe she said that, but he never denied the allegations of asking for sexual favors. Everyone I spoke with said the same thing: she had been lying. Nobody believed it, and eventually, we disregarded it as if she was lying. However, I never shared with anyone that I was always wondering if she was telling the truth in the back of my mind.

We got back from Atlanta and moved on the best we could; she stayed away from him, he stayed away from her. What I noticed is he was always trying to do the things his sons did. He loved the way they did certain things in their youth and wanted to keep that same flow going. During that time, I found out that my daughter and his middle son had become intimate. Was that the trigger point, I wondered? Was that why he pursued her in a sexual manner because his son did as well? I had a lot of questions, but I had no answers. I prayed and asked God to one day reveal the truth. Until then, we continued as usual as best we could.

June 2017, I started my church, one of my proudest moments. My daughter and I were the only attendees going every Sunday. He didn't attend; the church was not his thing. I knew that coming into the relationship, but I also thought he would support it since I started it.

> *I will say to every person out there, never expect a person to change just because you're doing something or you're married. Who they are in the beginning is who they will be.*

Nevertheless, it was my ministry, and I continued. I needed to buy a sound system for the church, and I found a company that would allow me to purchase these items for 90 days, same as cash. He allowed the account to be in his name, and each time each item was paid back in that 90-day timeframe. We made three purchases that way until we decided to get a card to pay monthly. Church had started growing and was doing OK. I wanted to move out of the hotel conference room. So we moved out of the hotel into a physical location within six months.

It was going well; it went from just my daughter to a couple of more families, and we figured we needed to be in an open space to attract more people. We went to a storefront building; services were doing well, people were getting blessed, and it was terrific. I had buried myself in the church because I was so alone at home. No one knew it because I masked it very well.

The church had become my life. They were my family, the people I hung with and the people I looked forward to seeing. I cried a lot, and no one knew it but every time I showed up people thought our marriage was perfect. I had a knack for that; I did that in all four marriages. The Church taught me, as a wife you never allow anyone to see that your marriage is having trouble. While I still believe that, you have to face your issues and talk to someone to get some help. The fact is, my marriage was the furthest from perfect. The man I was married to would rather sit in a room and play video games all day while I sit in another room and watch TV. Had this become my life, and how could I live like this for the rest of my life? Those were the questions I constantly had. Not to mention the sex was the worst. For the last three years, I spent almost every day having sexual relations with my husband while he interacted with porn on his phone. I was just an object for him to release while he was intimate with porn. It was degrading; I felt like an object. I would just lay there. I felt like in that scene from *The Color Purple, "I just lay there while he do his business"*. I remembered looking up at the ceiling, counting the popcorn in the ceiling, or settling the cracks in the house. I would see how many new cracks would be in the ceiling each time we has sex. Sometimes I would lay there and cry! It was heart wrenching , to say the least! But I lived by the Scripture that said "wives, your body is not your own but your husbands and husband, your body is not your own but your wife's". I was taught that early on, and that was the Scripture used to never say no to our spouse when it came to intimate relations. That kept me in bondage! So many times, I wondered why do we use Scripture to keep people in bondage rather than tell them this isn't right? Every day and night, I was very dissatisfied. No one would understand the pain I felt inside while smiling outside and pretending that everything was well. I was indeed living a lie! Out of all of my situations, I never knew one that could feel so good could feel so wrong!

On the one hand, he appeared to be the perfect husband, but on the other hand, it was horrific. I had everyone fooled, his parents and my family. They all thought we were perfect. Hell, sometimes I felt that we were perfect until I realized we were not! I had him overcompensate in some areas because of the lack in other areas. I wanted Lipo, he paid for it, I wanted jewelry, he would buy it. Whatever I would ask for, he would get it. The worst part was he felt like he paid all the bills, I should do everything he wanted me to do. While, I felt that because there was such a lack, he should do everything I wanted him to do. What we had was not a marriage, even though on the outside, it looked like it. We were an arrangement and did not even know we had entered one.

The worst part of it all was, I had lost my voice. If I voiced my opinion about how something made me feel, he would turn it around and make it seem like I was the one wrong. He would go so far as to get angry and sleep in the other room and not talk for days. I despised the silent treatment, so I just wouldn't bring up any issues to prevent that from happening.

I'm now working at a fitness gym, and it was the first job since I have been south that I absolutely loved. I love my connection with my team, members, and the community! I enjoyed being at work. Then, Covid happened! The world was greatly affected. The thing that kept me the happiest was closing down, and I had to be at home quarantined. I said when this happened, most marriages, churches, and businesses will not make it. I had no idea that I was going to be hit in all of those areas. He had begun as a silent partner with a restaurant that closed, my job shut down, and my church. Every day we spent all day in the house, I was miserable and suffered.

I thought it was "I'm just cooped up in the house". But there were moments that I hated my name to be called; I hated cooking three times a day. Needless to say, the weight gain behind all of the work that was put in has now gone to waste. I honestly thought we were going to be one of the couples that would be OK. But that was the furthest from the truth. I went back to work after one and a half months, and there were limited hours. I will come home early, 3 or 4 o'clock, because we were not open that late. Many people were not returning to the gym, so it made no sense to be there and open every day, all day. Although I was coming home early, I hated to be home. When the gym started picking up, that was my opportunity to work late and hang out there more. I would work out early and work late. Again, I saw myself spending more time there because I hated to be home. It even got to the point that I would get headaches when I got close to my house. I would sit in the car before going in for about 30 minutes.

It's now January and February, and gyms typically pick up. I was working late, training new staff, having turnovers, and filling in for other shifts. Although I was upfront with saying I'm working late, I was constantly accused of having affairs. When simply put, I just did not want to be at home! So I took the extra shifts, worked late, and was frustrated.

On the other hand, My Church was doing great. It was my outlet! Once we opened back up, of course, we lost members who did not feel it was safe to come back to church yet, but we gained some great new members. One of my members who worked for me started going to her old church while attending my church and I wanted to see what she was raving about. I remember it like it was yesterday, December 13. I went to the church in Jackson, Mississippi and sat in the back. It was an excellent service; they introduced me at the end, in which I had remarks. I remember the Pastor saying; we will come and visit your church; since you came to ours, we will be visiting yours. I left immediately and did not visit again.

About one month later, he made good on his promise, and he came to my church and enjoyed the service. The lady who attended both of our services asked me to sing praise and worship for her ordination service, the first Sunday in February of that year. I agreed, and we had a rehearsal with the Pastor. She and I rehearsed for that service with him the Friday before that Sunday.

We sat around after the rehearsal and joked a little bit, and she said, we can grow these two churches. You can come to her church, and she can come over here and help us out, and we can help each other and have one church in two locations. At first, we laughed, but then we said that it probably could work. He was a musician which I needed, and I was a singer which he needed. So we agreed to do just that after the ordination service. Could this be my outlet for Sundays? After all, I would get out of my church service by 10:30 am, and the entire day would just be wasted because I was alone! It was great while it lasted.

One Sunday in March, he had to preach somewhere else and asked me if I would preach at his church, to which I agreed! This would be the one day the snow decided to come down in Mississippi, and it was terrible. My members were coming, but some of them had to turn around; my daughter totaled her car because she slid on black ice. It wasn't good, but some of us still pressed our way. After the church was over, those who rode with me talked about the service, and suddenly my phone rang. My husband and I had been arguing for days, and I was terrified to answer the phone. I had no idea what he would say or how he would react, and there were people in the car with me. I answered the phone because I did not want him to think I was ignoring him.

*Hello! You are going to keep on until all of your shit is put outside!*

*Hey-hey, I have people in the car with me!*

He hangs up and calls right back,

*You are going to keep F*cking playing with me, and all of your shit will be outside.*

I said calmly *"OK, if that's what you feel necessary to do, go ahead and do so. I'll be there shortly."* This went on for at least two more calls. I had no choice but to answer it on speakerphone because the snow was so bad that I could not release my hands off the steering wheel. I was furious and embarrassed. But my members were great, and they both said that their husbands do the same thing and sometimes you can't calm them down. But this was different, and I knew it. He's blown off the deep end before but never like this. In our arguments, I also mentioned that he was taking care of his ex-wife, Still paying the mortgage, getting his full retirement check, and still listed on his military benefits as his wife! I had gotten so quiet that I was numb. I did not share that I was not satisfied. I also did not share about the things that upset me. I knew once I started talking about them that I was just about done with the marriage. I was giving it the benefit of the doubt with great hopes that it would turn around, especially if he loved me the way he said he did. Just fix this marriage, that's all I wanted. I was willing to deal with everything else that was wrong.

When I got home, we argued and argued and argued! There was no reasoning with either one of us at this point; we both just wanted to be heard. I usually back down, but this time I could not. He kept saying the Felicia I knew would have ended this argument by now. I knew then I was fed up; he said I was no longer on his team, but he was never on my team. Although he was the head of the house, I was very clear on the Scripture that said we were to be submissive to one another.

We have made women feel less than women with that Scripture telling them that they had to submit to their husbands when the Scripture says to submit to one another. I had become the footstool that I had fought so hard not to become. I remember sitting in the living room, and he said that I could see how spouses kill their spouses and then turn and kill themselves. Who did I marry? That was all I was thinking! There is no way that my husband would make that kind of a statement to me. I felt like the song that said there's a stranger in my house. I was in tears, my heart sank, and I was confused. I did not know if I should go or stay. But I kept remembering this is still the man I love and says he loves me he would not hurt me.

We argued so much that I went to bed with a headache. He came in shortly behind me and attempted to apologize, but I was too hurt to hear him! He started rubbing on me, kissing, removing my clothes, and I tried to hold on to a no without saying no. Still remembering Felicia, your body doesn't belong to you; this is your husband.

He pinned me down and forced me to have sex with him! I was in tears, just crying and crying, then he said, *are you cheating on me*? Over and over, I was crying more because I was hurt! When he finished, I showered and cried. I prepared to go to sleep with my gun under my head because I was scared. I didn't know this man! I told him, *you are like Dr. Jekyll and Mr. Hyde. I don't know who you are.* He rolled up with a strange look in his eyes and said, maybe I am. I knew it was another spirit operating, and I just needed to be safe, so I got quiet.

The weekend had come, and my goddaughter decided she would come down and stay with me. I didn't think anything of it because this always happens. Although he and I were not talking, I felt like I needed an outlet to get away from that pressure. She came and stayed, but he didn't come home. She and I had gone to the church and sang some songs to free my mind, and then when we came back home, we were getting ready to eat; she said, *have you seen the stuff that he is posting on Facebook?* *No, what is it?*

I grabbed my phone to look at it, only to find out I have been un-friended on Facebook by him. 10 seconds later, I was unfriended and blocked. *"Wow! I guess we are done,"* is what I stated. I continued on the day, and we retired for the evening. We woke up for church the next day, went to the first and the second service, and then returned home. About an hour after we had sat down to eat, he came in after not being there all weekend. He told her this was not a good time and she needed to leave. I told her, don't say anything. I'll see you later. After she left, we argued and argued and argued! We even got a mediator on the phone who saw some of the things his way and some things my way. Nevertheless, he said so many things to me and left me in a position that I could not move past it, at least not right then. He left because he had one more day in the hotel. He beckoned me to come but I refused.

The next day I went to work and came home, and he was there. It was on Monday, and Mondays are always my late days. I came home at about 9:00 PM; my head was hurting, and I was hungry. I sat down to eat, making minimal conversation, and then went to bed. He came back into the bedroom and began kissing and hugging me, holding me down as a mechanism to have sex. We are not in a good space for this.

*"Do you mean to tell me I can't make love to my wife?"* " *Not right now! We have been arguing way too much!"* " *I just want to make love to my wife. I just wanna be inside of my wife and feel you again."*

All while I'm being held and pinned down.

*"I did not call the police before, but if you force it today, it would be considered rape."*

I was physically kicked out of the bed and onto the floor. With tears in my eyes, I said, *"why are you doing this? Why do you keep escalating things? Why don't you allow these things to just die down? Just stop!"* I grabbed my pillow to go into the other room, and I know I heard God say just leave. I grabbed enough clothes for one day. I was packing things, trying to grab make-up, and crying at the same time. The next thing I heard was, *"get the F*CK out! Get the F*CK out! Why is it taking so long?"* The items I had put on the bed, he kicked them off and was throwing them around. *"Get the F*CK out; it doesn't take this long to get out; just get out get the F*CK out of my house!"* I finally left and got in my car. I drove up the street crying, and didn't know where to go. Finally, I went and checked into a hotel close to my job to sleep in a little later. I could not believe that this had become my life! The man I had been with for the last six years did what I thought he would never do! All I could do was cry myself to sleep, but I woke up throughout the night several times.

The next day I went to work, explaining to the owners and my immediate boss what happened. The owners decided to pay for me for the remaining week to stay in the hotel, which was four more days. It allowed me to sit and think about my next move. That Wednesday, he called saying I needed to get the car out of his name, and I said, fine, I can get a car today; that became an argument because he didn't understand why it was in his name in the first place. Nevertheless, I went to a car dealership to trade the car in. I informed him they might need you to sign a document since this car is in your name. *"Well, I'm not coming out there to sign a piece of paper; you signed everything else in the house just signed it."* I proceeded to trade the car and thought nothing about it, I signed all the documents and drove away with my new car.

I had to go back to the house to get some clothes because I would be gone for a week, and I only grabbed enough clothes for a couple of days. He stated he would be out of the house by the weekend, and I was supposed to be going back to stay at home. I guess that's how he saw where I purchased my vehicle because of the tags. Within the next couple of days, the dealership called me saying I needed to bring the car back because my husband stated he did not permit me to trade the vehicle in, and it belonged to him. *What?* I could not believe this. The car was only in his name because of a lower interest rate, but I paid the car note every single month. It was my car! I drove it! I had a white Honda accord, and he had a black Honda accord. I tried to call him to tell him that I would get another vehicle and he would be stuck with two Car payments, but he would not answer. I got to the dealership and met with the GM, and that's precisely why he said that they would just get a car in my name without the trade-in. As I'm sitting there, I'm looking out the window, and he's standing out there with the police. They told him that in order to get the car, he had to press charges. This was like a movie; I thought, what in the world is really going on? I didn't think anything of it; I left and went back to the hotel. Something did not sit well in my spirit. I woke up the following day to call the attorney's office and asked them to contact the police department to see if he pressed charges on me. Sure, as you know it, he had pressed charges on me, and they were waiting to see if the judge was going to sign off on a warrant for my arrest! I cried profusely. How could the man I married want to press charges on me for something he knew was not valid? However, the attorney said, *"No worries, we will go down and bond you out, and we will deal with it later."* It seemed like things got worse by the day. I could not believe the man that I loved was trying to have me arrested. He called later that evening, stating I will go and get the charges dropped the first thing in the morning. *"Why would you do that?" "Didn't I say that I will go and get them dropped? Why are you talking about it?"*

This is the way our marriage was. I could not speak about bothersome things because he never wanted to confront the issues. I always had to let them just be swept under the rug. But once again, I found my voice! I was no longer in a place of wanting to be quiet. We argued on that call for over an hour. We talked about everything from working late to him cursing me out, no support, hating my church, credit card debt; you name it, we talked about it! All for him to say, just come home.

The problem was I didn't feel safe any longer. Here is the man that forced me to have sexual relations, threatened me, physically kicked me out of bed, and now the latest pressing charges on me. I did not feel safe that he would be the protector any longer. Why would I want to be in the same household? At this point, I knew I would never trust him again. But I still loved him; I just was not in love with him, and I sure as hell didn't trust him.

The week in the hotel was coming to an end, and I was trying to figure out if I should go to a weekly stay hotel or try to pay this bill. This bill was $850 per week, and it would be hard for me to do it. I spoke with my Pastor in Chicago, and he agreed to pay for the hotel for the next 30 days! I knew God was looking out for me even in the difficulties of what I was experiencing. He would not allow me to come to the house to get any more clothes, so for the next 30 days, all I had was what I took out for the week. If you knew anything about me, you knew that my clothes were always a big deal. Check out some of my Facebook postings; it shows you exactly how much I feel about my clothes. Nevertheless, I smiled through it! I had enough clothes for work even though it was not my norm; I just had to continue to wash them to make sure that they were always clean. My church clothes, however, I did not have enough. I had not worn the same outfit twice in a year, but I did not have the money to purchase anything.

Some people that knew what was going on decided to help out in that area, and they purchased clothes from my favorite boutique and had them sent to me. Someone else went to pick up some clothes from the boutique, and she sent additional things free of charge. The only part about that was my weight was up and down. A lot of the items were a bit snug, but it was all I had. I wore them as if I had purchased them myself. I woke up every morning to minister "Coffee and The Word" to everyone on my FB live. I knew for sure they saw the giant thermostat on the wall, so they knew that I was not at home. Strangely, no one asked if I was OK if I needed anything or just a small conversation. I remember thinking these are people that I serve and serve well, preach to every day, prophesy to, help if needed, Have even paid some bills, and no one is concerned enough to ask me am I OK? There was a very small group with whom I shared things because they were leaders, and I felt like they needed to know for accountability's sake. But others seemed not to care until it became a big deal later. Nevertheless, I continued to do what I knew I was called to do.

One Sunday after the second service, I was hesitant to leave when I usually would leave right out. The Pastor said jokingly, what are you still doing here? You're typically gone. I broke down and cried and shared some things with him. He was attending my service, and I was still attending his and he had no idea. Shortly after, I started receiving food at my hotel, and I never knew who it was until weeks in. I never asked any questions; the front desk staff would call me to say there's a package at the desk for you. I had no idea who was contributing food, but I was grateful, and I knew God had sent an angel! Another employee and friend would cook meal prep food for me so I can stay healthy. I finally put it together and asked the Pastor was dropping off food boxes, and he said yes! He had a food pantry, so he donated food to me.

Well, my 30 days were up, and it was time for me to move into the apartment that I finally found someone to rent to me with these charges hanging over my head. But the apartment was not going to be ready until another three weeks. I had to remain in the hotel for another three weeks, this time out of my pocket, because I did not want to call my Pastor back and say I needed additional money. Finally, it was time for me to move into the apartment, and I was super excited. The only bad thing is after hotel expenses, security deposit, and first month's rent, I had no money to buy furniture. I moved in with only a few items I have accumulated while being in the hotel. I remember sitting on the floor with no TV to watch, no furniture to sit on, but I was happy that I was finally out of the hotel. The Pastor, who has become my friend, gave me furniture for my living room and a bedroom set. I no longer had to sit on the floor or sleep on the floor, and I was happy.

I said thank you and how excited I was to be able to have him as my friend. It seemed funny that those outside were willing to do more than those I was close to. But I continued and was thankful to God. It did not matter who he used as long as he used someone.

I remember thinking, what's next? My only reason for being in Mississippi was my church. I felt lost! I had no real friends that I hung out with, and it had become tough to be me. The Pastor and I started conversing more; he gave me an outlet to just cry or talk about my disbelief and where I was. I shared with him that I may need to find a roommate as things were very tight. My car note had just about doubled along with insurance. He said, how about I use your place to shower when you are not at home. I'm waiting at my house to get ready, and I'm staying in my building.

I'll pay half of the rent. He said many didn't know that he stayed there, and he wanted to keep it that way, but the water pressure is very low, and there's no shower. I knew that it would not look good if others saw him coming in and out of my apartment. But he had helped me so much and was offering to pay half the rent for the next month. I needed help, and he needed a place to shower. Who would see him coming in and out, I thought? I was so far away from my church, and no one knew me in this area. So, I allowed it! He was going through his own divorce, and I did not realize how messy things would get after this point. But how could I not help a friend who has stepped in and become so helpful to me? He would come in late nights after I had already gone to sleep or early mornings after I had already gone to work. We never really saw each other in the same space because of our schedules. The only day of the week we were there together was on Sundays. I would cook, and he ate dinner there. It was great to have someone to talk to because this was the worst "Situation" I had ever been in. I think I knew he was starting to grow fond of me but wouldn't say anything because technically, we were both still married.

<u>The next Sunday</u>, my daughter, during church service, went outside to smoke a cigarette. She came in and said, *"Ma, while I was outside smoking, dad pulled up and took pictures of the cars outside." "What?"* I was not preaching <u>this Sunday</u>, so I immediately got up and ran outside. He's gone, he left after taking the pictures, but he asked me if I knew where you live, and I said "yes!" He said "will you give me the address?" I said, *" No, I'm not going to give you my mom's address." "I will give you the game that you asked for if you give me the address. I'm not betraying my mom for a game."*

So he left. When she mentioned that to me, My mind went back to when she said he approached her and propositioned her for sex. All I could think about was this proposition the same? I'll give you a game, or I'll give you a computer if you give me what I want. It was at that moment I realized she was never lying! I felt bad, and I immediately apologized to her. I asked her then was she telling the truth about that? She said, *"oh, absolutely, I will never take that back, but I knew that I was lying a lot, and it put you in a position where you could not believe me."* I was hurt! What I am currently experiencing did not have to take place had I believed her story after it first happened. That probably will weigh on me forever. Nevertheless, I immediately sent him a text message saying I would file a restraining order the next day. I took off work the next day, drove to the court, filed an emergency restraining order in which the judge granted for ten days pending his response. I was new to this and have never been in any legal trouble, so I did not know the ramifications.

That evening I had an emergency meeting to meet with the leaders of my church. I was forthcoming and told them everything that I could think of at that moment. I left out one piece of information for a very good reason. It would force me to tell someone else's truth, and it was not my place to tell. So, I stuck with the details of only my story. I had experienced things, the arguments, the abuse, the charges being pressed; you name it, I told him everything. As a couple of days went on, I started getting phone calls one by one after the other members said they would pull back from the church because it was too much. I didn't argue with them, nor did I even ask for the details; I just said OK. Because what I understood is that the situation has become too much for me, so I knew it was too much for them to deal with as well. One member went into detail and stated that the Pastor who played bass guitar for me, his ex-wife, had reached out to her, stating that he and I were having an affair and living together. My heart sank. Although I was somewhat devastated that someone would believe a complete outsider over their Pastor, I still did not argue with their decision. The thoughts that were going through my mind were, "are you even going to ask me my side of the story?" At that moment, I would have felt obligated to tell the complete truth. But I was too hurt even to comment.

I accepted the resignation and wished her well. I got another call from a couple of other leaders that stated they had gotten the same message that this other member had gotten. And that she stated she had proof. This member said *"Pastor, what do you want me to do?"* because I did not respond, nor did I open it. Because I knew I was innocent, I responded to her and asked her for proof. When she did just that, the other person got defensive and said, since you don't believe me, forget it. I won't send you a thing. Of course, my member said that's exactly what I thought you had, and even if you did, that does not mean I will turn my back on my leader. Not that I expect anyone to have my back when I'm wrong but give me the benefit of the doubt as I had done for so many of them. This was a hurtful place to be in. I have prayed for people, labored with people, paid bills for some, went to the hospital with some, heard of the things they were dealing with as far as staying in their lives, and was not given the same benefit of the doubt; this was so hurtful! I know some reading this will probably say, but you were the leader you were expected to have higher regard. I understand that I was not expecting not to be expected to be different; I was expecting to be heard out before concluding. Nevertheless, I continued on. I decided to meet with everyone one on one and not in a group setting.

Those that had decided to leave had also now begun to spread the lies as if they knew as a matter of fact that they were true. The absolute truth was this Pastor had become an excellent friend when I had no place to live. I stayed in a hotel for eight weeks, and he made sure that I had food. When I finally moved into my apartment, I had no furniture because my husband would not allow me to take anything. He made sure I had furniture in the living room to sit on and mattresses to sleep on. It was nothing extravagant, but it was more than I had, and I was very appreciative! So when the time came, he was living in his building at his church, and no one knew that. The building did not have a shower; He needed me to be the friend to him that he had been to me. Unfortunately, his house fell through, and he was devastated. I was out of funds. I had no idea how I was going to pay the bills that were coming up. He asked, and no matter how it looked, he needed help and so did I. He also asked if he could park one of his vehicles outside permanently because the building had just gotten vandalized. Because this person helped me so much, I could not just say no in his time of need. What I am sure of is the church people are the main people saying and praising the fact that Jesus was unorthodox and He did things that the Pharisees and the Sadducees did not want Him to do. He healed the sick; He hung out with the sinners; He did whatever was unorthodox to get the work done. But the minute we, as modern-day Christians, do the same type of thing, then we are ostracized, ridiculed, and pushed away. Although I knew it did not look good, I needed help, and so did he. Little did I know that his ex followed him to my apartment and started scouting the area out. She took pictures and circulated them to my church members. Her pictures included his cars outside of my apartment building. She began saying they are having an affair.

Due to the number of people that had decided to walk away from the ministry, I knew that we would be in trouble financially. I had a decision to make, and I needed only God to help me make this decision. I met with people individually via phone, via Zoom, and FaceTime to decide the fate of the ministry and for them to hear the conclusion of the matter. One thing I know is that the Bible says to judge with a righteous judgment which means a complete assessment. That means you have to hear it from an honest perspective, you have to listen to the entire conclusion of the matter. I wanted everyone to listen to the complete conclusion of the matter and hear it from me and not the lies as they were being told. I still was not at liberty to say he was living in his building, so I said he was my roommate. That was the furthest thing from the truth. I gave the information that he was renting a room from, and he never slept in a room in my apartment. Could I have handled it differently to get a different result? Absolutely! But that involved me telling what one would consider failure in his life, and as a friend and Pastor, I would never do that to anyone.

I had two more members to speak with, and I did that on Friday and Saturday. Friday, I talked to a lady, and she was very sweet, and I knew she was very hurt. To this day, I love her dearly; her spirit is incredible; what I appreciated about her while she waited to hear the conclusion from me before making her decision. That is all I asked from anyone to listen to the conclusion and then make your decision, and if you decided to walk away, all we can say is all would be well. The last person I spoke with was my musician. He had usually been very well mannered and respectful, and I could not meet with him with everyone else because he was working, so I sent a message saying for him to call me if he wanted to hear it all from me. I was at work getting ready to start a meeting with my staff on a <u>Saturday afternoon</u>, and he called. I stepped away from my meeting to speak with him because it was that important to me. I began sharing things with him as my partial truth. Immediately, with a very disrespectful tone, he started saying to me how he felt that it was not right and even stated that my attire was so tight and didn't even dress like a pastor. He proceeded to say that he told someone that when I put oil on others, that I need to put that oil on myself and get delivered. I was in shock that I could not even say anything to him. I held the phone back and said, listen, I'm just going to be in prayer for what the next is. He merely said do you want your church because I want to be there if you want your church but if not, let me know so I can make some other moves? I immediately responded I absolutely want my church. I started this church with my blood, sweat, and tears and not one member, so I do not wish just to give it up to come this far. He said OK, well, I will be there tomorrow, and we'll see where things are from there.

This was a Mother's Day Sunday, and I was not preaching on that Sunday; my assistant pastor was. As usual, I did praise and worship; and this time, the musician was very late. I signaled for him to come on up, and we continued on with praise and worship. He usually has the mic, and he sings with us. This particular Sunday, he kept his mask on and did not sing at all. I wasn't going to argue with that either because my singers and I are used to just singing with each other before him. After the sermon, I had the media department put a logo up on the screen that said refocused. I announced that what we were going to be doing over the next seven days was praying.

We were all going to go on a sabbatical and take this time to hear from God. Sunday morning service would be via Facebook live done by my assistant pastor. I announced this had been a challenging and trying week for me. I have been lied on, accused of things, told everything down to how unfitting my clothes were. When I said that part, my musician immediately just threw up his hands in disbelief that I was stating that. However, I never said who said it and exactly what they said. I was telling my truth and the hurt that it caused me. Once again, I felt had anyone asked me what was going on, they would have known why my clothes changed. The fact of the matter was my husband had stolen all of my clothes, shoes, jewelry, make-up, purses, coats; you name it, it was all gone. The clothes I had been wearing for the last couple of months were all given to me. I was surviving the worst situation experience that I have ever had to deal with. I had absolutely nothing, and no one took the time to ask what was going on. The number of tears that I dealt with, the hurt, pain, and agony, was over-whelming, to say the least. Not only did the man that I had just spent the last six years with destroy everything that I owned; he destroyed the relationship with the people that I loved most and spent all of my spiritual time building up. They were not even in tune with me enough to inquire what was going on; sure, one or two said, Pastor, do you need anything? But no one said what is going on. As pastors, the fact of the matter is that we suffer as much as the people suffer, most times greater. However, we can't show that we're in a situation because we're too busy dealing with the people's situations and their issues and their pain. I admit I am very strong, but this was breaking me, and no one asked *"what is happening"*!

That Sunday, I went on to the second service of the Pastor that played bass for me; that was a trade-off; he played bass for me; I sang for him and his church service. We both had very small churches, and we were helping one another grow. While I was sitting there, I got a noti-fication that I was tagged in something on Facebook. I never go on my phone while in church service. But I knew that God had orchestrated me this way on this day. I opened Facebook to see that my musician had posted a video, and he tagged me in the video, and he was dogging me out in such a way that was slander. I did not watch the video; I immediately untagged myself and then blocked him. At that moment, I did not know what it said. Later I found out all of the accusations that my husband had told my church is what he was saying in the video; however, he was saying them as if he knew they were true. I lived in a small town in Mississippi; all it takes is one rumor to ruin you.

I went on my sabbatical, praying and asking God what to do about the church. The funny thing was when quarantine hit us in 2020; I thought I heard God say close the church and go completely virtual. Because the average small church will not last or sustain this. We were online doing Covid and had gained some members while online. When we went back into the building for the first time, the church could take care of itself. I thought maybe I heard God wrong. I understand that when you don't do the things that God say to do, he allows a situation to force you to do it. Especially if you ever say, "not my will, but your will be done." After that video had gone out, I knew there was no way we could return to the church in that town and not the same way.

I remember a very close friend and preacher texted me saying, "God still loves you, and He never stopped!" She shared some other things about when God allowed her to be exposed, which changed her life. She continued on and said the man I was with was not my NEXT! I waited about an hour before I responded with the truth; I was physically kicked out of my bed and home, and the "man" that everyone is speaking of was a friend that saw a friend in need and decided to help. Not one time was I judged by him; he just became a friend with no questions asked. I was surprised that my friend did not take the time to ask what was going on and how she could help. Instead, she jumped to conclusions and believed the rumors my husband started. What made it worse, she barely knew. I was torn with the fact that he was able to call my Bishop, who he didn't like, and now my friend.

My Bishop called me for a meeting when my husband asked, but didn't say much to me when I reached out at the onset of our problems. My friend's husband went to my home to meet with my husband to "help." He was able to get the attention of all of the folk that mattered to me, and I was sitting quietly operating by the Scripture that said vengeance belonged to God. I felt hurt and let down. These are the people that could call me to preach at any time. I would pray and prophesy to them, so where was my alliance? Who would check on me to make sure I was OK?

It felt like my world was crumbling and all the pieces were landing on me. Everyone I knew was turning their backs on me. It was clear I did not do everything 100% correctly, and I allowed some things that would help others get in front of my priorities and duties of my church and life with God! As time went on, this same friend continued to send me messages to join her virtual services. I got tired and lost it. I finally responded with "I live by the quote that says, 'people don't care how much you know until they know how much you care." The fact of the matter is, and I say this to the "CHURCH," we attempt to feed the world our God without making sure that the world is OK. Even Jesus met people where they were... When they were hungry, He fed them; when they were naked, He clothed them. Have we lost our compassion and only want to preach what we consider truth down the throat of others? I didn't lead my church this way and indeed didn't deserve to be treated this way by so-called friends.

I continued with the plans and met with the remaining members that Wednesday, and we decided to strategize our next and if we would continue online. I decided I would sell everything in the church and sublet the building if I could find someone because the church had $2500 on a credit card that was solely in my husband's name with me as an authorized user. I wanted to owe no man nothing, especially him. I was willing to sell about $30,000 worth of sound equipment, musical instruments, chairs, soundboard, you name it, for a little of nothing just to pay off that debt.

That Monday, I had someone who wanted to look at the building and all of its items. I had a member to meet them there, and when they got there, low and behold, they said, pastor, none of the instruments and Mics or sound system are here. I said, what? They were just there on Friday! I immediately said, don't worry about it. I knew my husband had these things. I urged to call and make a police report. Little did I know when the police got there, they stated he had called the station and said that someone had broken into the church and he was taking his items out so they would not steal anything else. He was that someone! He had stolen everything out of the church, only leaving the furniture. I had the hotel across the street look at their cameras to tell me what time and day this happened. He didn't know that we were not going to have church that Sunday. He had broken into the church, took every-thing, left to call the police and had them meet him there. He did all this on a Saturday in hopes of ruining our Sunday service. It was apparent to me that everything he was doing was to embarrass me. He wanted to publicly humiliate me. He had gone too far! He attempted to get me arrested, stole all of my personal belongings, destroyed the church, and now he had stolen everything out of the church. He wanted us to walk into the church on that <u>Sunday morning,</u> prepared for worship and find nothing there to use to make service work. He also informed the police that he had stolen it. The police stated I needed to go to small claims court since it was a civil matter and there was nothing they could do. Once again, he was doing everything he wanted to do, and I was sitting, saying, God, you said vengeance belongs to you, but I'm being destroyed little by little day by day. The fact of the matter is, he was trying to make it seem like he was doing this because one we had the joint credit card debt that, according to him, he knew nothing of. He also told them that I was having an affair. Both of these were so far from the truth. The truth is, I had spent $25,000 on a restaurant investment that went bad because of him. He then reported all of the credit cards as fraud and when they realized they were joint cards, they told him it could not be a fraud. My bank account information was there to pay these credit cards automatically, but the information was removed at the report of a fraudulent claim. Now they were expecting him to pay, and he was not happy with that. He was trying to destroy me, and it bit him in the butt.

The next day, I went back down to the church to grab some items that I could personally use. We had four large televisions, all of them were gone at this time. He was taking things out one by one each day at a time. The following weekend I came back to get a couple of more things, and all of the chairs were gone. I had 154 chairs; how do you take this many chairs, and where do you take them? Lastly, all of the office furniture in four offices, including mine, all had furniture, and now they were all gone.

I talked to my mom daily! She was the one person that I could just let out my frustrations and how it was affecting me. Because once again, I'm expected to be strong, I'm expected to hold my head up, and I'm expected to fight through this. But I have gone through a lot, and this was devastating. During this time frame, I lost my father; I was now losing my marriage. I had no personal money; I was evicted from my home, and my church was being destroyed. The one thing that I built is now gone. This all seemed like a movie, and it was turning into a nightmare. How could one person endure so much and still expect to survive? I was still a General Manager of a fitness gym; therefore, I couldn't quit. I need to stand and be strong. Although I was losing so much, there was so much I still had to keep pushing for.

When those around me found out I was going through this much, they asked, "how are you still standing?" I would look at them like a deer in headlights because I had no answer except by the grace of God. The good thing was I moved down the street from where I worked. When things began to get too overwhelming, I would take a break, go home, cry, pray, and just sit and stare and then return to work with a new attitude. I had a lot of those days, that's how I kept my sanity.

Things started to die down. As my mother would say, well, what more could he do? I would just laugh out loud because in the beginning, every time I would make that statement, it seemed like he would find so many other things to do. So I stopped asking those questions and just started living each day by day. I still felt pretty much alone even though I had my job and my team members who were constantly asking me if I was OK. It still felt like I was alone. The funny thing was that those on my job seemed to be more concerned about my well-being than those I was connected to for years, especially those in the church. By now, my pastor friend and I began talking more and spending more time together because it seemed like no one would understand what we were going through but us. His ex-wife and my soon-to-be ex-husband had yoked up and they were determined to destroy us by any means necessary. It was one thing after the other, and it was unbelievable. We have a great friendship at this point and learned to trust each other. Someone asked me if I would consider dating him, and I said I did not know if I would ever look at another man the same. But what started happening was his friendship allowed me to see that he was a good and misunderstood man. I did not realize it, but his friendship was keeping me sane. Had I sat in my apartment by myself day after day, I probably would have lost my mind. I am convinced that God allowed his friendship with me so that I did not feel alone and isolated as I was beginning to feel.

We began to do a lot together, hang out with groups, sit around and play games, eat and just have natural fun to take our minds off of the foolery that was going on around us. Things were quiet, and I liked the newfound peace. That is until the big next tragedy happened. I know you are probably saying what more could happen next. A group of us decided to drive down to the coast and stay a couple of days and just hang out. As we were driving, I got a message on Facebook from a publicist, or so they said. He asked if I was the pastor from Vicksburg? I responded yes, and he said *"I just want to give you a heads up; you are being accused of cheating with a pastor and multiple men in the city, and it's getting ready to be a full tell-all on you."* I responded *"with, what? Where did you get this? And it doesn't matter because I'm not."* He sent pictures of me exiting my apartment and my pastor friend entering my apartment on the same day but early in the morning. This was during the time that he was coming there to shower. I laughed and continued. He continued to send me messages trying to get me to talk to him; he had some local live show where he reports what he considers scandals in the town. I would not give him the satisfaction of the day by responding to him. But later on, he made a post on his page with those pictures, another picture of a car door being opened for me, and another lady. These were the same pictures they had given to my church at the beginning of March, and now it's June. They had absolutely nothing new but continued to spread the same old things. His post said everything from we were having affairs with multiple people and orgies in our church. I was absolutely ready to fight. I cried, and I cried, and I cried. How much more could I take? How much worse could this get?

My oldest daughter had a legal program that allowed us to send cease and desist letters. They were sent to this publicist, my ex, and my friend's ex. That did not stop them from sending that post out to everybody in the world. My ex was adamant about making sure that whatever he felt was his truth and sending it out to all of my family, friends, coworkers, and you name it. By this time, everybody was tired of his foolishness. Of course, the community, who did not know us, but reveled in having bad things to say. Unfortunately, the church rallied around those same posts and joined in the negativity. But those that knew me said if they had just left it at the affairs, we probably would believe them but now to add all of this and they are continuing to add things; we know this is not your character. It still does not mean that I was not hurt; I was probably more devastated that someone who once said they loved me would go to these lengths. Someone I knew reached out to the "online gossip publicist" and said you should not be putting these types of things out on an educated black woman. He promised him that he would not make another post about them and would like to let it go, but the damage was done.

The recovery from this to keep me sane was the gym. I worked out every day with a smile on my face, and I never let anyone see that what they were doing was getting to me. I went home, and I cried, screamed and kicked most days. I don't even think that I was the nicest person to be around. My pastor friend probably took most of the heat. Not just because his ex did a lot of this damage but because he had become the closest to me. I don't even know why he is still my friend because I became evil at home. I felt like I had no purpose. Ministry had been my purpose for so long, and now that was stripped. Where do I go from here? How do I pick up and start all over again? It was starting to get unbearable. One thing I knew for sure, God was on my side, I should have lost my mind. I allowed my assistant pastor to do all of the preaching for our online services; I prayed a lot, I sang songs of Zion, and some days I sat in pure quietness and did nothing. I still wondered where "my friends" were. Not one text, not one phone call, you name it, nothing. But I was determined to make it. I love the Scripture that says he will prepare a table before you in the presence of your enemies. I started declaring and creating every blessing that I knew God had spoken to me. I did what the Scripture said according to Isaiah, and I commanded his hand to move. I started commanding and proclaiming that things were going to turn around. That cease-and-desist letter didn't hurt either, it seems like it's slowed them down. I believe they were still doing some things, but they were not bothering me.

I was just ready for the divorce to be final and to be completely done. You would think I've been through this three other times. I know what divorce is but this was not normal. This one had the tendency to take me completely out had I not been rooted and grounded in my faith. What kept me? My faith! It was not the people around me; it wasn't food or money, but my faith! Oh, and consistent exercise. I would post pictures of me exercising every single day; I posted pictures of new outfits that I had obtained during this time since everything was stolen from me. I would not give the enemy the satisfaction of thinking that he destroyed me; I needed him and others to see that my God was well and able to deliver me out of this.

On the other side of things I realized my pastor friend and I had become trauma bonded. So much had taken place that we depended on each other because the same things were happening to us both. We hung out daily, went to church functions together, hung out with friends, and eventually grew fond of each other. Once the trauma died down he and I started disagreeing often. We started having unnecessary arguments that we had never had before. The truth was, we were connected and bonded by trauma and once the trauma slowed down, the arguments increased. We realized we did not know each other at all and some things we liked about one another but it was more that we didn't like. One day the argument was so bad that we decided not to ever speak again, we came back around and took that back but I realized the trauma was the thing that kept us close.

This time, I stepped back and had a serious conversation with myself and said *"Felicia you are headed into another situation and if you do not pull back this would not be good for you."* It wasn't that he was not a great guy, it was the timing of it all and we were not ready. I was not healed! I remembered sending a message saying "I have to take care of Felicia"! I'm giving too much of myself to this and not taking care of me. Fact of the matter is I no longer want to be in a relationship that was started because of another situation. I'm OK being alone! I'm OK toughening things out and figuring out my next, just with me and God the way that it should've been in the very beginning. I love my life too much to let it be led by situation after situation!

*I'm fighting for Felicia!*

**Journal Entry**

- When was the last time you stepped back and had a serious conversation with yourself? Have that conversation and jot down your revelation.
- What are some questions you wished you would have asked before or during a relationship? Jot them down so they next time you feel this way, you can be reminded to ask the tough questions.
- Identify 3 genuine friends or prayer partners you can trust. You will need them when life gets rough.

# SITUATION 7

*THE DISAPPOINTMENT OF IT ALL - Church Hurt*

As I reflect on each situation, it was more than what I experienced that was a lesson. Still, it was the disappointment and hurt behind it all, especially from those considered my leaders and my friends.

In situation one, I will never forget sitting down talking to my then Pastor, explaining to him the nature of my divorce. I was attending his church faithfully in which I was a praise team leader, youth leader, and I had started the arts ministry (dance and drama.) In addition, another leader in the church was beginning his church, and I was helping them out in the afternoons. When my Ex and I could not get counseling together because my husband decided he no longer needed counseling, I met with the Pastor to tell him I would be moving forward with the divorce after the second stage of abuse. He stated, "I hate to hear that, and I'm going to have to sit you down for a while." I was so devastated. I had done so many things in this church and because I wanted to divorce my abusive husband, the church looked at it as sin and took it all away. I remember the Pastor of the afternoon church questioning his decision to sit me down. He did not ask him, but he posed the question to me and began sharing his disappointment. He stated he did not believe that should have been the decision based on why we were divorcing. Why didn't he ask the Senior Pastor? I have no idea, but the decision devastated me!

How could a man take something from you that God gave you? These were my God-given gifts; how do you get to determine when I use them? But I did not argue, and I did not fight. I came Sunday after Sunday hurt that I was no longer being used. This lasted for some months until the New Year's Eve service. The Pastor approached me and told me I could start being active again; it blew my mind. What do you mean start back being active? You have stripped me, and now you want me to jump up and do things because there is a need. I made an appointment to meet with him the next week because I was sure that my time and season was up at his church. But before that, a young lady that was very promiscuous had gotten her breakthrough and said she would no longer live that way. A couple of months went by, and she was doing well, and then we found out that she was pregnant. The baby came as a part of what she did before changing her mindset and no longer wanting to live like. She had asked God for forgiveness. She was up singing and ministering to others, but now, she was being sat down as well because she was pregnant. When I met with the Pastor, I said I was not meeting on behalf of my issue although he apologized and said he was highly sorry maybe he should not have sat me down. No one had ever gotten a divorce in his church before, so he did not know how to handle it. That did not change the hurt that I experienced! But I said to him, how do we know that people live a particular life and allow them to work in the church, but then when that lifestyle is evident to others in the form of pregnancy, that's when we want to sit them down. I said many people Get hurt from churches from this entire "sit down, OK … you can get back up" process. Who made us God?

During situation 2, you may remember me saying I got married to save face for the church. The interesting part is that when that Pastor found out I was pregnant, I still sat down. I'm not saying we should sin so that Grace could be abounding; I am saying that if we all had to sit down for wrong things, there would be no church. So what gives us the right to make a judgment call on someone's life with God is the ultimate judge and is in a position to forgive us all.

In situation 4, there was no disappointment from a leader's perspective, but the frustration came from others in ministry and those who were my friends and in church. It all seemed like no one knew what to say. It seemed like no one knew how to deal with me. When I got completely healed, everybody started to talk to me again, saying "we didn't know how to respond." This was a divorce, not a plague. Where is the restoration? You know the part in the Bible where it says to restore one in the spirit of meekness! Where is that one? How could we spend so much time preaching and teaching to others but not know how to deal with those closest to us?

All of a sudden, the people that used to ask me to come and preach weren't asking me to preach. Why in the world is it that the church, which is supposed to be the love of God, inflicts this kind of pain on people when their situations have already caused them enough? I remember one church in particular that used to ask me to come in minister a lot had an event coming up, and it was suggested to have me as the speaker. Someone had a problem with it because they said, what could she tell the young adult ladies coming up? I thought that was the most bizarre statement. What do you mean? I can tell them not to make the mistakes I made and how essential it is to wait and not get caught up in situations!

The ultimate amount of pain happened for me in situation six. Friends that I consider close were no longer calling or texting. There were times we would share laughter videos using Facebook, that stopped. Friends became very judgemental based upon what they heard instead of asking how I was doing? I had leaders that my ex reached out to and shared his side with that reached out to me after speaking with him. Not to mention that I had already shared my issues. The initial hurt behind all of this was adding to my disappointments. Lastly, it was my church family, except for a few that jumped on the bandwagon.

How could it be that the very people that I was pouring my life into were now ostracizing me?

I know I mentioned a lot about the church, but it could be anyone close to us. Those closest to us tend to judge the most and become the most hurtful people, especially when we are going through our most devastating moments. One would think that those that are closest to you would extend love to you during that time. I spent many days agonizing over the pain I had from those that I considered my friends, leaders, and pastors. Shouldn't we be asking ourselves, "am I my brother' s keeper? "We all have a charge to keep, and that is to make sure that those around us are healthy and happy as well. Tabitha Brown makes a statement after every one of her live posts, and she says, "go and have yourself a great day and even if you can't, don't you dare go messing up anyone else's." Such a powerful statement! We have a responsibility that gives us a charge not to mess up anyone else's day. We shouldn't ever want our brothers or sisters to leave our presence hurting. Whatever you can do to make sure those around you stay healthy, if it's within your power, do it!

**Journal Entry:**

- What are some things you have learned even in your disappointment?
- I am learning on this healing journey that I never want to hurt anyone and cause trauma to their lives. What are some things you identify with that would cause you to change the way you treat others?
- There were a lot of things I didn't share or feel comfortable sharing early on that could have landed my healing earlier. Think back over your life, what are some things you could have shared or received therapy from that could have avoided some of the pain?

# SITUATION 8

*OVERCOMER*

After being asked so many questions like why so many marriages? How did you go through all of that and come out sane? When most are having a hard time finding a boyfriend to commit to, how did you manage to get eight rings? When I sit back and ponder those types of questions, it makes me say, wow! You do not realize how bad the trauma is while you are going through it. As I began to put my pencil to the paper, I started to rehash all of the events that had taken place from the time I was 20 until I was 53; I have to say, I endured a lot. After everyone else's questions, the questions I had for myself were "what did you learn so that you would not end up in the same place again"? "What advice will you give to someone else so that they don't have to go through what you've been through?"

Those moments are when we must take a hard and close look at ourselves. The subtitle of this book is the enemy in me, meaning the enemy within. I don't want to look at what everyone else did to me or what was done around me. I want to look at what I could have done differently and what I learned so that I will not end up here again. This last situation taught me to stand still and see the salvation of the Lord. At the end of every breaking point in my life, I would pack up and move. Sometimes in the same city and sometimes far away, but I would move. I wanted to move this time, and I heard God saying no! I was offered a job out of state, and I could have moved, but I heard

God saying no. What was I going to do differently? I am going to be obedient, I am going to sit down and listen, and I am going to watch all of the signs and what they are showing me.

At the beginning of every situation, there was something that I saw, but I ignored it. There was also something I needed rescuing from. This time, God was the only rescuer I wanted and needed. This is hard for most of us because we have a plan A, but just in case plan A doesn't work, we also have a B, C, and D. But being still and trusting in my God was the new place I found myself. I know you're probably saying, how could you not trust in God if you are a preacher? There was a father in the Bible that brought his son to Jesus to be healed. Jesus asked him did he believe. His response was, "I believe, but help my unbelief". As much as we love God and live for Him, there are those other times where we have unbelief. Giving up complete control is hard but necessary!

Things were terrible after each situation! I had to file a couple of bankruptcies, pick up the pieces and figure out my finances. I also had to change jobs until I figured out what would sustain me. But I would not change anything that has taken place in my life because each situation got me to this point.

I started trying to write this book after situation 4, and it was not time. I knew a book was to come out of this, but I didn't know when. This isn't a book to tell you how to trust in God, this isn't a book to belittle men, and it sure isn't a book to glorify the fact that I've had four failed marriages. However, this book shows so many that are in a situation, have been through a situation, or currently going through a situation that you can heal from trauma.

I had to smile in the face of adversity. I had to smile when I was hurting. I had to smile when I wanted to give up on life. A lot of what I've done in the past as a healing mechanism was for the benefit of others. I had children, a mother, a grandmother, a father, or just people who depended on me, so I could not afford to give up. This time around, I'm doing what's best for Felicia! I needed to get healed and whole for myself.

So, you ask me what is it that I've learned and what I would do differently? I would say I would focus on myself! I would take care of my mental state, and I would do everything within my power to make sure I was successful and did not need to depend on anyone to rescue me from any situation.

I found my voice! I had lost my voice way back in situation one when I was scared to say how I felt. Even though I gained some things out of each situation, I still had no voice. The problem was I did not realize I did not have a voice. It wasn't until situation 4 when I realized that I was becoming everything he needed while losing myself. Sure, I gained some material things, sure, I gained a house, a car and clothes but I was physically and emotionally empty. I regained my voice! I am not afraid to use it. That's why I'm writing to you today to speak to so many people that have lost their voices. To talk to so many people that are sitting and saying to themselves, what now? Get up! Get out of that chair, off of that couch, out of that bed and stop sitting in the car for hours before you go in the house. Oh yes, I'm talking to you today! This is the time that you get your fight back. Not your physical fight but your fight to regain your life, regain your power, your position, and your voice. You deserve that! You deserve to be the best you that you can be.

I know someone is reading this and probably crying because I'm shedding tears as I write it. I feel the pain that you are enduring today! I feel the hardship that you are enduring. I feel the burdens you are carrying, but when you fight your way out of this trust and believe me, you will have tears of joy. The Bible says "weeping may endure for a night, but joy comes in the morning." I do not know how long your nighttime will last. I don't know how long you will have to endure the pain before you get on the other side of this, but if you fight for your-self, you can see a new day coming soon! The Bible says in 3 John 1:2, *"I wish above all things that you would prosper and be in good health"* There were times at the end of each situation I felt like I was having a heart attack. I thought that my escape from those situations was causing so much pressure that I was dying. This life can make you feel so bad and beat you down that you start feeling sick or that something fatal is happening to you. Take your life back, my sister! Take your life back, my brother! You deserve to be healthy, happy, and whole!

So what now?

I want to talk to the little child in you who grew up without your parents. There is a familiar scripture that says *"Honour thy father and mother; which is the first commandment with promise; that it may be well with thee, and thou mayest live long on the earth."*( Ephesians 6:2-3 KJV) For whatever reason, that parent or those parents were not in your life. Yes, it has left you hurt. Yes, it has left you feeling alone. Yes, it has left you with a void. But it does not have to end there. That Scripture is a perfect reminder that we are to honor them. What does that honor look like? For some of you, your parents chose alternative lifestyles over their children. It could have been drugs, alcohol, prostitution, and for others, the parents simply just were not there or had to give them up for adoption. Either way, you were without your parent(s). The honor you place on them says I honor them so much that there is the part of them that was not good for me. I honor them for showing me that they were not the best parents and allow that to teach you how to be your best. Whatever your best is, whatever you are reaching for in life, you place honor and high esteem on them to be the best version of yourself that you can be without holding anything back.

This is the time that you get to step back and look at everything that failed you and say, I want to be greater than that. You must choose to break the cycle. I'm reminded of a sermon that my pastor friend recently preached, and it said to ask God for the forgiveness of your forefathers, meaning your parents, grandparents, great grandparents. Why? Because there are things that they did that are trying to spill over to your life now. How do you break the cycle? How do you break this generational curse that allows itself to be attached to you? You stand up and declare that you're going to be your best and you're going to live your most extraordinary life without fear and without holding back. My mother had me at 19. I had my oldest child at 19. I had to get to the point that I broke that cycle. I did not want that for my children, so I began to pray to break those generational curses. You owe this to yourself and those coming up behind you. Hold your head up, square your shoulders, plant your feet and declare to the loudest point of your voice and say I'm going to make it out of this. This thing will not get a hold of me, but I will have a hold of it.

Next, I want to speak to the person that keep finding themselves giving to the wrong people. A portion in my writings stated I had become a wife way before I was a wife, and I became that for people who were not deserving of that. I cooked, I cleaned, I pushed them to their purpose! Just because God has equipped you to be who you are, does not mean the vast majority of the world is ready to handle that. I know that The Bible says a man that finds a wife finds a good thing. We have taken that Scripture out of context. Somewhere down the line, we have allowed ourselves to be told that the man has to find us, and when he finds us, we marry him, as if we don't have the right to choose to be found. Just because he does the finding doesn't mean you have to give in to what he found in you. If he does not deserve you, don't give yourself to him. Men, if she does not deserve you, don't find her. We are not obligated to give ourselves to anyone but our God. You deserve to live your best life! Many won't understand the following statement, but it is OK for you to be selfish. *"The blessings of the LORD, it maketh rich, and he addeth no sorrow with it."* (Proverbs 10:22 KJV) It's OK to be selfish to better your growth and your health and LIVE your best life!

I also want to talk to the person that keeps accepting abuse. Scripture says: *"What? know ye not that your body is the temple of the Holy Ghost which is in you. which ye have of God, and ye are not your own?"* (I Corinthians 6:19) Protect your temple! If it's mental, protect your mental state. You do not have to accept anyone speaking badly to you. You do not have to take anyone beating you. That is not what you were made for. Take a look at yourself in the mirror, go ahead, do it right now and tell yourself how great you are, tell yourself how wonderful you are, tell yourself how full of purpose you are, and then look at yourself and smile and say YES, I am all of that! YES, I am better than what they said! YES, I am going to be all that I can be! Get up; you do not have to take that. Do not allow church pressure, others, and anything anyone will say to make you stay in a bad relationship full of abuse. A child is looking up to you, saying, is this what I should expect in a relationship? Be better than that; you are better than that. GET UP and walk away! You are nobody's punching bag!

Lastly, I want to talk to the person that continues to make decisions out of fear of what everyone else would think. No one has to live your life but you. Don't let what others say to you or about you cause you get to decide what is not good for you. Sometimes we stay in things for fear of what others would say. Sometimes, we continue doing something because of what we told others. It's OK to say I made a mistake! It's OK to say I thought I heard from God, but didn't. It's OK, to say this was not right for my life, and I am moving on. Fear, which is said to mean: **F**alse **E**vidence **A**ppearing **R**eal, can hold us captive. The Bible says *"For God hath not given us the spirit of fear; but of power, and of love, and of a sound mind."* (2 Timothy 1:7) I speak that to you today. Walk in the power that was given to you! Experience the love that God has for you! Live in peace with the sound mind that you were made to have. This is your time to live for you! And it does not matter what others say, think, or how they look at you. Live your best life! Don't fall captive to bad situations!

It is my hope and prayer that upon reading this book, you get free! You get delivered! And most of all, you get healed! It is your time to live your best healthy life and live it full of purpose. You deserve this time. Let your latter be so much greater than the former.

Now do me a favor, "Gone Get Yourself Some Healing" ....I believe I will!! SITUATIONS

# YOUR HEALING NEEDS

**Time and Preparation**

- To change your life, you will need to change your mindset. How will you prepare for your healing journey ahead?

  What are some things you need to change that will require you to mentally accept first?

**Independent of everything that was held as high regards as if it was needed.**

- What things/people can you separate in order to pursue what is really needed in your life?
- It wasn't until I fell apart that I realized I was living for everyone else except me. What are some things you can do to put the focus back on YOU?

**In your Pain is when you are to push to your purpose.**

- How has this thought provoked you to see yourself as purposeful?
- There are two ways to be happy: change the situation or change your mindset. In your journal write out where you see yourself headed and the pain that caused you to see that you had purpose.

Then write out the plan of action you will now take to get to that destination.

# SITUATIONS
## THE LIES BENEATH THEM ALL

Written By: Felicia Lynette

https://Linktr.ee/FeliciaLynette
FacebookGroup: Refocused
Instagram: @felicialynette_refocused